I0791327

YOUR LIFE EXPERIENCES WITH RAH

UNTOLD STORIES

"HIDDEN TRUTHS"

RAHUL K. MAHARAJ

authorHOUSE

AuthorHouse™
1663 Liberty Drive
Bloomington, IN 47403
www.authorhouse.com
Phone: 833-262-8899

Published by AuthorHouse 07/28/2022

ISBN: 978-1-6655-6700-8 (sc)
ISBN: 978-1-6655-6702-2 (hc)
ISBN: 978-1-6655-6701-5 (e)

Library of Congress Control Number: 2022914076

Print information available on the last page.

Any people depicted in stock imagery provided by Getty Images are models, and such images are being used for illustrative purposes only.
Certain stock imagery © Getty Images.

This book is printed on acid-free paper.

*"Trust is one of the Hardest
Things in this world to gain,
Trust is also the
Easiest thing to lose."*

Rahul K. Maharaj

CONTENTS

Dedication ix

Acknowledgment xi

About the Author xiii

Preface xv

New Year's Day Surprise 1

Not Sure What I Am 5

My Angel Sent by God 9

The Mechanic's Son 13

Supergirl 16

Side Chick 21

Real Nightmares 25

My Wife and BPD 30

My Stepfather, The Beast 36

My Mother Stole Her Mother's Husband 43

To Believe in Something You Never Knew About 48

My Father 52

My Father Made Me His Wife 57

Mother's are God's Angels on this Earth 63

Love Rape Relationship 66

Last BBQ 73

I Named My Daughter After My Best Friend 77

Family Secrets 82

Family Christmas Spirit 86

Dangerous Game 90

Betrayal with a Price 94

Angels Do Exist 99

Never Ask For Too Much 102

Fat Sweet Bottom 106

Your Life Experiences with Rah 117

DEDICATION

"Your Life Experiences with Rah '' would love to dedicate this book to all those who have been through some hardest times in their lives, as this is the preordained destiny of every human being who is born on this planet. The minute you are born the struggle of life begins. For some, the challenges are breathtaking and never-ending, and for others the challenges of life are very simple, but keeping up is just not something they are mentally built for.

I would like to dedicate this to all those who shared these stories. They are brave and showed their courage to share one of their life toughest moments and how they overcame it.

"From where you were to where you are today."

Always do some retrospect and see from where you were in life to where you are today. No, I am not saying to dwell in the past, but rather to look at challenges from the past you thought were the hardest or toughest and to see how you have overcome them. In the same way, whatever the situation is, it will be over soon since everyday is a new beginning for you.

I want to thank all the beautiful people who shared with me their life experiences which are being depicted here in this book without revealing their real name. Hence, This book contains no real life person's name and information. And all the names which are being used here are totally fictitious.

Though all the stories are invariably the "real life stories of struggles" taken from the life of just a sample of people. So, you can get to know what happens in the lives of millions.

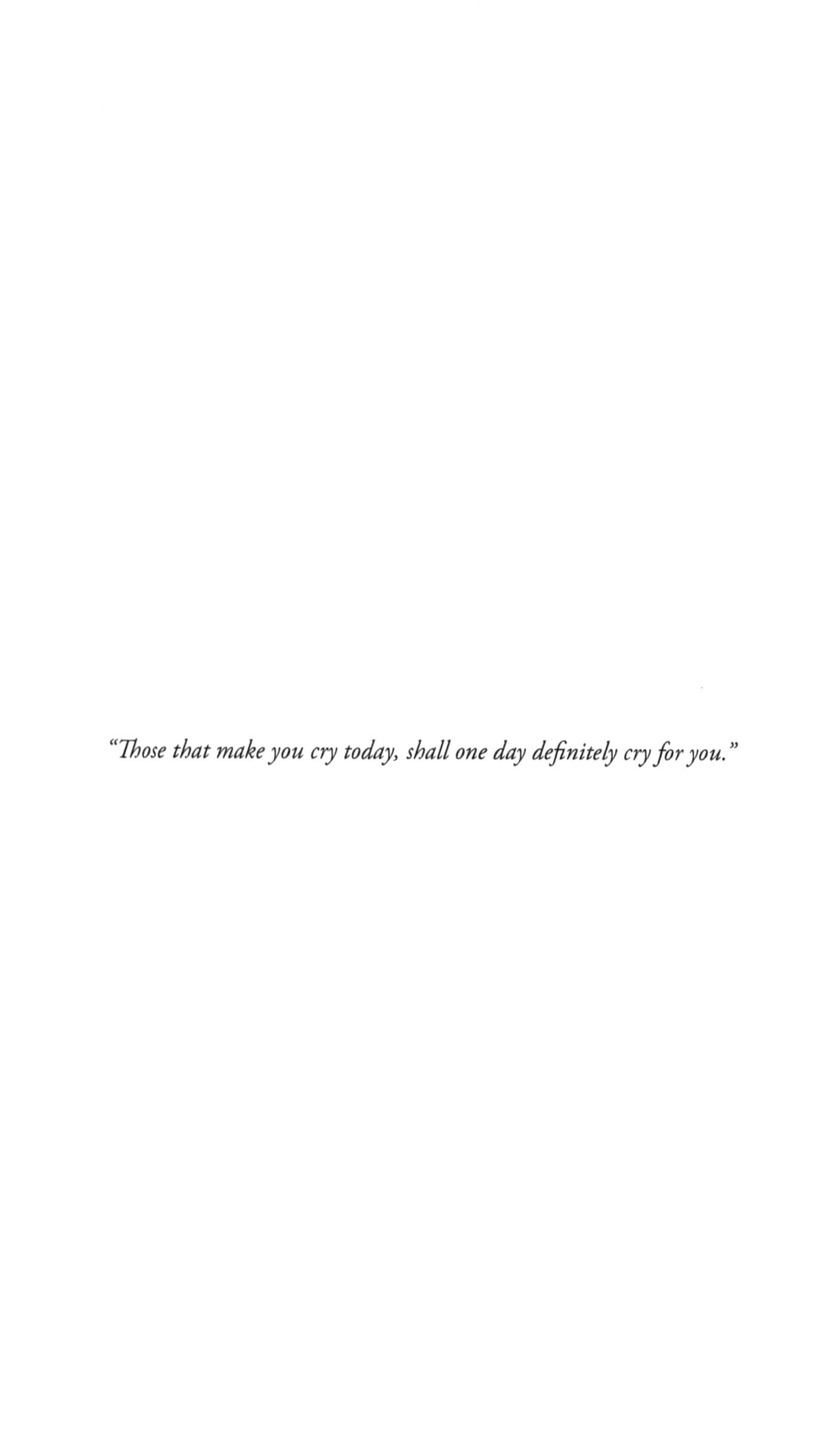

"Those that make you cry today, shall one day definitely cry for you."

ACKNOWLEDGMENT

Given this opportunity, I must tell every single one of you that you are not alone, and *'your mental health' is* nothing to be ashamed of. Mental health problems affect and in some cases destroy millions of lives every year. Someone somewhere is struggling with some sort of Depressed Mental State that no matter how hard they try they just can't overcome easily.

Acknowledging all those who shared these heartwarming, heart touching, heart wrenching real life stories with me, I would like to thank all of them as readers will be able to relate and know that they are not alone. I know it's hard. I have been through dark phases of my life like you all as you all might have heard on my show *"Your life experiences with rah"* or soon to come in one of my upcoming books on *"Rah's story"* coming soon. I can relate in many ways. I can't say I have been through some of these things, however, and I thank God for only giving me what I can handle and hats off to all these amazing people who shared their stories. I know and I believe if I can do it, you can do it too. I know it's easier said than done but if you read some of the traumas some of these individuals have been through and how they overcame or how they pushed forward and did not dwell in the agony of the past, I believe you all can do it too. I believe that a lot of things play a part in different types of mental disorders. I believe that the lives of others, whom you are part of, play a huge part in your lives, especially those of you suffering from mental health disorders. I want you all to once again know you are not alone, and that this is not happening to only you.

Let's acknowledge all those with the following Mental Health Disorders and Problems.

Anxiety disorders, including panic disorder, obsessive-compulsive

disorder, and phobias. Depression, bipolar disorder, and other mood disorders. Eating disorders. Personality disorders. Post-traumatic stress disorder. Psychotic disorders, including schizophrenia.

Anxiety and panic attacks.

Bipolar disorder.

Body dysmorphic disorder (BDD).

Borderline personality disorder (BPD).

Depression. Dissociation and dissociative disorders.

Drugs - recreational drugs & alcohol

Last but not least PTSD (Post-traumatic stress disorder).

"I would like to thank my best friend ANA NICOSIA for all the help in editing and restructuring these stories so that these wonderful messages of life's struggles can reach those who need to hear them. Please share your comments and views about these stories and feel free to contact us YLEWRAH@GMAIL.COM and send your story or come on the show and share your story live."

ABOUT THE AUTHOR

This is the author's short success story of how he, Rahul K. Mahraj fought to become one of the most inspiring personalities ever.

He migrated from Trinidad and Tobago 21 years ago as an immigrant. He started working on the second day at a Children's store in E Flatbush in Brooklyn, then moved to a sneaker store a few days later doing what he needed to do to make a living. Coming to America with basic education and computer skills, Rahul knew he can do way better with the right opportunity at hand. That opportunity came about a year and half later when he landed into a job at a construction company as the manager.

He worked his way up, later on moving on as a financial advisor where he helped families to have financial stability. He also worked hard to help others repair their credit. He opened his own daycare to provide a loving, safe and stable environment for parents to leave their "little angels" during their working hours.

Having suffered a lot of hardships during his life, Rahul found that through telling his stories he could encourage people to open up about their difficult experiences and give them a voice to share their stories with others. He travels across the country in order to raise awareness about mental health issues and help anyone suffering from any kind of mental illness. Rahul wanted to approach the problems associated with mental health in a unique way so that the path to mental wellness is made easier and approachable for people.

This also led to him starting his own YouTube channel called "Your Life Experiences with Rah" three years ago where he talks about everything that he went through and also talks to his followers about various issues as well as teaching them to meditate and deal with different hardships in life.

He has been working as a mental health speaker for over 11 years now as well as occupying the position of Chief Executive Officer of Little Angels Daycare LLC since 2014. Rahul became a member of the website called "THE BASH" in 2021 where people book him as a motivational speaker for both in person events and virtual sessions.

In addition to his work as a motivational and mental health speaker, Rahul also has valuable experience dealing with credit repair due to his time working as a financial advisor.

One of his most meaningful accomplishments is his show on social media *"YOUR LIFE EXPERIENCES WITH RAH."*

This show has been mainly started to help people open up about their mental problems and depression. It is a safe place for people to share their stories so that others can also get to know how to overcome such anomalies. In this way, people can come together to talk and to share, but most importantly to heal.

This is just a short story of how he started and where he is now. Was it hard? Yes - at every stage of life. Was it worth it? Yes 100%.

PREFACE

This book is for everyone since mental health is a vital issue not given nearly as much attention as it should be in society, and because many people refuse to even admit to themselves there may ever be something "wrong" - that they may need some sort of help or at least someone to listen to them. These amazing souls are crying out inside. Some with smiles, others with frowns on their faces where smiles never reside. While some carry the biggest smiles on their faces but bleed deep within, others pour their hearts out to the wrong people - and we end up losing these beautiful souls to Mental Depression, Clinical Depression, Suicide, etc.

Your mental health includes your social life and well-being, your emotions, and your psychological state of mind. All of this adds up and affects how you think, how you feel, and how you act as well as react. It also helps determine how you handle stress, how you relate to others, and the choices you make.

In this book you will read stories and struggles of others whom you don't know. You may ask yourself while you put yourself in their shoes: *"if this was me would i be here to tell this story?"* or *"hats off to them as i can relate to being in a situation that was challenging and i am still here fighting this battle called life."*

In the story *FAT SWEET BOTTOM* you will read about a father selling his son for a bottle of Johnny Walker.

In the story *Last BBQ* you will read about betrayal.

In *NOT SURE WHAT I AM* - **We were still on the couch and in a very sexual position while moaning in great pleasure as I opened my eyes to look up and see my wife staring down at us in such shock and disbelief as to what she was seeing** - think about what the wife would

"

have had to endure during that moment and what she went through or still is going through because of that shock. (PTSD)

While in the story *SUPERGIRL* - **Shall I start talking about the unconditional love my parents gave to me? Or do I just say once up a time and start the story like that? Why don't I just start off like this, my story is about a love triangle. There were three friends; two guys and a girl who loved each other equally -** this life story can teach humans so much about true love and sacrifice.

"Always put yourself in someone else's shoes before casting judgement."

NEW YEAR'S DAY SURPRISE

Hi Rah! Thank you for Your Life Experiences with Rah as it has allowed me to share my story with you today. It was on New Year's Day of 2015 when my world came crashing down.

It was about 12:30pm in the afternoon when there was someone knocking at my door. When I answered it, there was a man holding a baby girl in his arms. He was looking for my husband who wasn't in the house. The man at the door had a very mixed British accent. He asked if he and the baby he was holding could wait inside for him as it was very cold outside. I allowed this man inside my house while I called my husband. He was in the supermarket with our sons and said he will be reaching home in fifteen minutes or so.

As I sat down next to this man I looked at the baby girl he was holding. She looked up at me and the first thing I noticed were her beautiful hazel eyes. They reminded me of my husband's eyes. The stranger looked at me and said *yes*, those beautiful hazel green eyes you are looking into are your husband's eyes and this is his daughter. My legs got weak as I fell back. I couldn't believe what I was hearing. How is this true? I was in complete shock. My husband of twelve years and we are having two handsome boys together, ages ten and seven had cheated on me. How? When? With whom? This baby looked about two years old. Why am I just finding out about her now?

The man saw how confused I was and told me everything I wanted to know. He told me that the baby is his niece. His sister recently lost her battle to cancer and passed away a few weeks ago. He further explained that his sister was diagnosed in her second trimester of pregnancy and because she was pregnant, she refused chemo or any sort of treatment. The doctors had told her they most likely could stop the cancer, but she was too afraid it would hurt her daughter, or worse kill her unborn baby. He also explained that he was now his niece's legal guardian, but he got a job that requires him to travel and so he could no longer care for the baby. That is why he came looking for the baby's father.

I was still in shock hearing this man's story and at the same time my heart went out to him knowing this little girl was the only living family that he had. I knew he didn't come to my house to break up my family. I could see how much he loved his sister and her daughter and just wanted to make sure she was safe and loved prior to accepting the job that was offered to him. I had a million more thoughts and questions when I heard my husband's car pulling into the driveway. My husband walked in with grocery bags in his hands when he locked eyes with the stranger and the little girl. He dropped the bags as he was in shock about who was standing in his living room. The stranger just started to tear up when he saw my husband and explained that his sister had passed.

I thought I had been shocked enough for the day when all the sudden I saw my husband and this stranger kissing! Kissing in front of me and my children as if we weren't in the room with them. So now how can I forget that my husband had an affair with some woman and how I did not know about it. I was so confused and was beyond lost with all of my emotions. I just screamed out and demanded to know what was going on in front of my eyes when my children ran towards me. I asked them to go to their rooms and not to worry. Once they were in their rooms I turned to my husband and demanded answers but it was like I wasn't even in the room. The strange man was holding my husband's hands and leading him to the baby's stroller. He kneeled down to take the little girl out of her stroller and handed her to my husband. As he did that, he told my husband that they finally had a child together.

Again, I was even more shocked! What was happening? I walked over to my husband and grabbed the baby from his arms. I needed answers which I deserved atleast. My husband turned to face me and apologised. He never wanted me to find out about his secret affairs. Turns out this was far worse than I thought it was as my husband's story went back years, to the time he was a teenager. My husband and this stranger met when they were teenagers and fell in love. So now I'm thinking who did I marry?

Why would he bring me into this if he knew he was gay? Why would he allow us to have children and bring this into their lives? My husband asked me to remember where he came from. His parents were military and very religious. They would've never accepted their only son being queer.

My husband continued to tell me his story. He said he hasn't seen the stranger since they were nineteen. So now I'm thinking, ok then where did this baby come from and how does the stranger's sister fit into this story. So, my husband told me on one of his business trips, he met this woman. They had a few drinks and conversation. One thing led to another and they ended up having a one-night stand, never realising that the woman was the stranger's sister. This is when the stranger came into the conversation to fit the rest of the missing pieces to this puzzle. He explained that his sister told him about her one night stand a few weeks later when she found out she was pregnant. However, she never reached out to my husband because she knew he was married and had a family. She didn't want to break up his family. The stranger tried to get his sister to reach out to the man that got her pregnant, but she refused. When the baby was born, he noticed her hazel green eyes and knew this was my husband's child without question.

It's now three years later. I had to adjust to all that fell on my shoulders a few years back: Knowing that my husband was gay even before we got involved. Him never confiding in me about this and then bringing our two sons into this mix. On top of which my husband cheated on me with another woman that resulted in a child. I ended up losing my job and missing out on a lot of things with my sons due to the depression I fell into after all I learned on that New Year's Day. Prior to that day when that stranger knocked on my door, my husband and I had been trying to get pregnant again in the hopes of having a little girl. Unfortunately, there were complications which resulted in my hysterectomy. I knew this poor baby girl wasn't at fault for what she was born into and gradually I fell in love with her just as she was my own child. After all, I was her only mother figure now.

As much as my life was turned upside down on that New Year's Day it was also a blessing. I ended up getting a daughter I always dreamt of having. Yes, biologically she wasn't mine, but I loved her just as though she were my own child. It's true what they say, sometimes the blessings you receive are in a disguise.

In terms of my husband's sexuality. He admitted he loved the stranger, but that he wanted to stay with me and our children and raise this little girl together. We will make sure our daughter knows that she wasn't a mistake but a miracle in our lives. When she is old enough to understand, we will make sure she honours her mother's memory. She will know just how much her mother loved her, so much that she died for her. She will know that I wasn't able to carry her and that her mother will always be an angel in our eyes because she gave us what I couldn't.

Our daughter's uncle got married to another man and is happily married. He is very much a part of his niece's life as he visits her often. Everything sets into place as it should be.

Happy New Year's Rah. I hope your show will reach the appropriate audience so that they can learn from each other's stories. Wishing you all the best in 2019.

Cheers from Oregon

<u>IN THIS STORY, WE HEARD EVERYONE WHO WAS INVOLVED IN THIS AND THEIR SIDE OF THE STORY.</u>

People will think in many different ways, but you must put yourself in every situation and consider how everything happened and what was done. Was it right? Is there a right and wrong way to handle a situation like this? Should she have quit her husband? Should she have abandoned an individual child she had always wanted? were we concerned about her children? yes, her husband was wrong for cheating, but he also gave up a lot to change his life, and in life, we all make mistakes. some people continue to make mistakes that will no longer be a mistake but will become a habit. Life is so strange at times that we all need to know how to wear that shoe correctly.

YLEWRAH

NOT SURE WHAT I AM

Hey, Rah! I love your show; it's very inspiring. I also like how you incorporate your own life into Your Life Experiences with Rah. I heard about your story of how you were cheated on during your Valentine's special. I feel that you are very brave and genuine; however, I don't think you have moved on from that hurtful experience that you had to endure. After hearing your story, I am also comfortable enough to share my own story with you now.

I questioned myself over and again, if I am gay or bi or just chose one person of the same sex that I trusted enough to experiment with. I still don't have the answers as to what my sexuality is. I just know what I have done is what I was comfortable doing at the time.

I was born in Guyana and lived there till I was thirteen before I moved to New York. I started High School and learned how to adapt in the big and busy city of New York when I was just a teenager. I met my friend, Stephen, when I was in High School. He became the type of friend that I could always count on for anything. Even after High School, we remained good friends and both stayed in New York while attending college.

Stephen got married before I did, but that never affected our friendship. Even after I got married, we still remained close. We would still go on our "guys trip" to, for example, DR, Vegas, Costa Rica even after we both had children. Our wives knew how much we values our friendship and never tried to get in the way of it.

While Stephen and I are very close friends, we also shared a mutual secret together. We started to experiment with each other sexually shortly after we became friends. Does that mean we were gay or were we just in fact experimenting? Stephen is a very manly person and therefore he will take our secret to his grave! It's also another reason why he only did these things with me and never with another man. I too have only experimented with him and never another man.

I am now a thirty-nine-year-old man, happily married with two teenage children living on Long Island. I am a VP at the company I work for. I worked hard to get to where I am in my company. During your Valentine's Day Special, I believe you had your first Q & A? You gave advice to a person with gay feeling to be honest with his family and to tell his children the truth. You told him if his family truly loves him, they will not disown him. I thank you for that advice as I had to put that to good use with my children.

Last May, when my wife and children went off to work and school, I stayed home from work that day since I took a single day leave. Stephen came over as he, too, had a single day leave from his job. We had drinks and just caught up with what was going on in both of our lives. After we both got a few drinks in us, Stephen started to kiss me and before I knew it he threw me onto the sofa and we went at it. We were all over each other, kissing, touching and moaning from the ecstasy we were both feeling. We were in such heat, that neither of us heard the front door open. We were still on the couch and in a very sexual position while moaning in great pleasure as I opened my eyes to look up and see my wife staring down at us in such shock and disbelief as to what she was watching. I immediately pulled away from Stephen to console my wife, but as she saw me walking towards her she just put her hand up for me not to come any closer. Stephen begged her not to call his wife and tell her about this. She just looked back and forth at both of us as her eyes filled with water and then stormed out of the house. I will never forget the look on my wife's face. I shattered her heart that day. She trusted me with her whole heart and that day I broke it into pieces. That was also the last day Stephen and I ever saw each other.

My wife needed a few days to herself to collect her thoughts and herself. After she did, I tried everything to try to make sense of what my relationship with Stephen was and why I had kept it a secret from her for all these years. The truth was I still didn't have the answer, so I could give an honest answer to her. She saw the pain in my eyes and could see how confused I was and realised I had been hurting just as much as her. She hugged me and told me she is willing to work on our marriage and put this behind us, if I was willing to. Rah, without watching Your Life Experiences with Rah I think I would've lost my wife forever on that ominous day.

After that I worked really hard at making my marriage work, but it wasn't easy as a lot of mixed emotions from both of us were still hanging around. I took my family to Lake George for a vacation. Our children knew something was off with us as they heard their mother insult their father for the first time. We made it to Christmas, but just barely. We were in Chicago and things had turned a lot worse between us. At that point I still hadn't told my children the truth about what was going on. I remembered how you gave advice to be open and honest with your family, including your children. So I sat my children down to be honest with them and to explain what my relationship with Uncle Stephen really was about as my eyes filled with water from the shame of what I did and how it affected my family. Both of my kids just looked at me and hugged me. While they were hugging me, they told me that they love me, even if I am gay. I told them I didn't feel gay even though I had sexual relations with their uncle. I told them that he was the only man I had been with and that it was just part of that friendship. I told them that I was in love with their mother and that she is the one I wanted to spend the rest of my life with. My wife heard all of this and she just came over and embraced me with a hug. She told me if everything I just told our children were true, then she was willing to really work on saving our marriage.

Thank you Rah for your show, for your honesty, for your advice and for having a part in saving my marriage and my family. I know you not only helped me, but I am sure you have helped a lot of other people because of Your Life Experiences with Rah. Good luck, my friend. I hope you reach your goals and dreams to one day have your own studio and hope to see you on television soon. Blessings to you, Rah.

> *"I have seen and heard so many of the above stories with different scenarios. Recently I met with someone with a similar story. His wife caught him as well years ago while the kids were young. similar words and promises about only wanting to be with his wife, just to be caught several more times before they would actually get a divorce with lots of*

hate and malice. Once again everyone lives through similar situations in life with different endings or different directions.

In the above story you have to really put yourself in this woman's shoes and feel how she felt. go deep into how far along. maybe see if she still to this day sees that scene in her head like it's happening right in front of her once again. I have said this many times to many of my friends who have done this or are doing this to a female or male: "think about how the person will feel when they find out or in this case see with their own eyes." they will be broken. you don't know what you will do to that person or the mental state you will send them into. I will request you all to treat others the way you want to be treated. you must love yourself before loving others and love others the way you love yourself and want to be loved."

YLEWRAH

MY ANGEL SENT BY GOD

Hey, Rah. Has anyone ever told you how amazing you are? I wanted to thank you for taking the time to read people's stories as well as mine. After I heard the story about how angels do exist (the one where the girl was raped by her stepfather), I wanted to share my story.

I grew up at a very young age. I wasn't given the opportunity to have a childhood as my mother was too busy dating man after man rather than parenting me. As much as I had always wanted a sibling, I was very happy I was an only child. It would've killed me to watch any siblings go through what I did.

It started when I was about twelve, with one of the many men my mother allowed in the house. This one was different and not in a good way. This one got my mother on drugs. This one changed my mother's life and mine forever that night. I had woken up to use the bathroom that evening and, on my way, not only did I see my mother have sex with her boyfriend, but there was another man there as well. I kept my head down while walking towards the bathroom. I knew what was going on was none of my business, so I kept walking till I got inside of the bathroom. While I was in there, I thought of how I could get back to my room without anyone noticing me. I finally took a deep breath and opened the door and grasped at the sight of who was in front of me. My mother's boyfriend had been waiting for me with a devil of a smile across his face. I just put my face down again and said excuse me as I walked back to my bedroom. I thought that was the worst of it till I felt someone forcefully push me onto my bed and rip down my pyjama bottoms. As he entered me, I knew from his voice that it was my mother's boyfriend raping me. Anyone who has been raped knows all about the fear and how horrofic it can be. It is way too painful for me to write down the absurdity of things which happened with me as I'm worried that it will definitely hurts anyone reading my story or who had been raped.

I thought my mother would will come and save me, but she was too high to know what was going on. She neither saved me that night nor she ever tried to stop such instances happening with me again and again not only with that boyfriend but other men too that came into her life later. She would watch these men drug me so that I couldn't scream or move when they raped me. Rah, how would you watch your own child be drugged and raped night after night and not protect them? This is a question I will never get an answer to.

It continued to get worse. One evening she got so sick of looking at my face that she threw me outside into the winter's cold. I didn't even have socks or a winter coat on. I took the cover of the garbage pile to shield me from the cold wind that was blowing even colder that night. I was out there for seven hours straight before she came looking for me. At age sixteen I was diagnosed with HIV and at the same time found out I was pregnant. With whom, I never knew? You've read my story so far and know it's not because I was a slut. In fact, I never had consensual sex as all of those men had raped me. My child was born out of this horrific aftermath. The doctors watched my pregnancy closely and gave me medication so that I didn't pass my HIV to my unborn daughter. I thank God every day that I didn't pass it onto my baby girl. As much as I wanted to keep her, I knew I wasn't in any condition to be a good parent. I wanted only best for her and the only way I knew how to give that to her was to give her up. That was the hardest thing I had to do, but I knew it was best for her. I prayed every night that she would be adopted by beautiful and caring parents. I learned years later that my prayers had been answered and she was growing up in a loving home. I missed her everyday but was so thankful she had the childhood I never had and by giving her up I was able to give her that happiness.

I had been back on the streets as I didn't have any family to turn to. There were times I went without food, times I had to sleep in the streets in very cold weather. I had fallen so sick at one point that there were boils and sores all over my body.

One night, an angel appeared before me while I was asleep in the streets. His hand reached out to mine and he told me to come inside. I had been sleeping outside of his building. I don't know if it was because I was sick or cold or just really tired, but when I looked into his eyes I knew he was a man I could finally trust for the first time in my life. He allowed me to shower and even had fresh clothes for me to change into. He even dressed all of my boils with antiseptics. Turns out my angel of a stranger was a doctor. I never had anyone took care of me and wasn't quite sure how to accept it. I didn't want him to think I was ungrateful, because I wasn't. But how do you react as an adult to someone taking care of you, if you never had someone took care of you when you were a child? We talked all night. I don't think I ever had an actual conversation with anyone in my life. He told me about his sister and how she committed suicide three years ago. He felt all this resentment for not being able to save her. When he saw me, he told me all those feelings had come back to him and how I reminded him of his sister. He felt that if he could help me that somehow he was helping his sister even though she was no longer alive. The clothes he had given me were hers. He never had the heart to get rid of them.

He noticed how hungry I was and gave me food. My emotions were all over the place. Like I said, all of that had been new territory to me. In my life any man that came into my life wanted to take something away from me. I kept on trying to figure out what this man wanted from me. I tried to eat but I lost it as my emotions took over. I just all of a sudden started to scream. I was asking what he wanted from me? Why was he being so nice? Telling him that I didn't deserve his kindness? Was he being nice to me as a game before he raped me? This man just looked at me, kneeled down and slowly put his hand on my face to wipe away my tears. He told me all he wanted to do for me was to take away all of my pain and for me to allow him to make me smile.

He even took me to the hospital where he worked to get myself treated for HIV. He also had a friend who got me employment. He told me that I could stay with him as long as I liked and needed to. Well it's been fifteen years now and I still live with him. We are happily married. We have a life I never knew could exist.

I work as a social worker helping people like me. People who have been emotionally and/or physically abused. I also help people when they are diagnosed with HIV. I share my story with them to give them hope. To show them that one day the storm will be overTo not feel like they don't deserve to be happy. Everyone deserves to be happy. Unfortunately, there are evil people in the world that make us feel differently.

My husband and I adopted two beautiful children. We gave these children a life their biological parents couldn't. It makes me think of the child I gave up, but I know I wasn't in a position to give her the life she deserved. I never wanted to raise my baby in the streets with me.

When I look into my children's eyes, I sometimes ponder about my mother. Not about where she is today or if she is even alive, but how she let drugs and men come over me. That is something I will never understand. Children do not ask to be born. God gives them to us and it is my belief that it is a sin if we put anything or anyone in front of them. Our children should always come first.

Rah, you, too, are always in my prayers every night. Please continue to do what you do.

In this story, I put myself in her shoes and I couldn't do it. To be honest, as strong as I am, I applaud her for her strength which she kept on carrying with her. I have seen people going into a depressed state "which is all ok" for "small problems". Let's think about what this innocent soul has been through. There are some of you fighting your mother who cares and loves you unconditionally. While this child also wanted that, some people do get things easier than others and the sad part is they don't appreciate what they have until it's too late. by me saying it's too late, i am not trying to say until that person passes away. oh no, i mean don't let the way you treat others catch up to you. it does come around 10 times worse. you better be strong enough to handle your karma. i always say love others the way you love yourself and the way you should love you.

As I said before, I applaud this woman for her bravery and her drive to survive. i applaud her for not letting the things in her past hold her back from seeing that after the storms of life there is always a rainbow to show that hope is near - as she put it "angels sent by god".

YLEWRAH…

THE MECHANIC'S SON

I would like to begin by telling you how interesting I found this show-"Your Life Experiences with Rah." It's been six weeks and I am hooked! The stories I heard not only touch my soul but they even made a man like me cry. I loved the stories presented on your show even though the same are anonymous which somewhere down the line inspired me and made me comfortable enough to share my own story with you.

My family and I were born and raised in the Caribbean. My father has been a very ignorant and proud man. I grew up watching my father aggressively beating up my mom almost every single day. I would think it wasn't right that my father would hurt my mother like that. I told myself that if I were ever blessed to have a good wife by my side, that I would worship her and my hand would never cross her's or any woman's face for that matter.

Surprisingly, nonetheless the horrible husband and father he was, he was an amazing business man. All of his customers loved him and his works. I couldn't understand why my father didn't treasure my mother. She supported him in all odds of life but rather than worshiping her, he made her feel worthless as hell. My mother gave birth to my two older sisters. Even this thing upset my father because she kept on giving birth to daughters instead of sons. When my mother got home from the hospital after having their second daughter, my father beat her because my sister wasn't a boy. He acted as if my mother intentionally didn't want to honor him with a son. Why couldn't he understand that the sex determination of the children is out of any woman's control? I guess if he knew that then my mother wouldn't have been abused the way she had been.

My mother suffered two miscarriages before she had me. Rather than my father comforting her when she lost her babies, he beat her and called her a failure because she couldn't give him up with a son. Years later my father got what he deserved as he lost both of his legs in an accident. Unfortunately that accident just took his legs and not his life. I know that sounds harsh, but how could I love or have any kind of respect for a man that brutally beat up my mother over and over again for being a good woman?

When I was twelve I began to work and save the money that I had earned. My parents didn't even know that I had stopped going to school so that I could work. My older sisters found out that I hadn't been going to school but they didn't tell my parents. They feared that our father would abuse them the way he did our mother. Plus, they knew how much I hated school and they were protecting me as well from our father.

My father's friend owned a mechanic shop. He saw how good I was with cars, so he allowed me to work for him. He taught me everything I know today. It had been four years since I had dropped out of school to work in the mechanic shop. My father found this out when I was sixteen. He was so angry that he picked up a 2x2 piece of wood and beat me with it. While he was beating me, I screamed what a coward he was and how he wasn't a man. A real man would never lay a hand on his wife or children. That just made him beat me more and harder. Somehow, I got that piece of wood from him and raised it above my head. I was about to hit him with it when I realized if I did, then I would be just like him, a man I never wanted to be. So instead, I dropped that piece of wood beside him and left that house without ever looking back.

I once again asked my father's friend, the mechanic, for another favor. He allowed me to stay with him that evening. The following morning, he had a big heart to help me. He wanted to expand his business and in order to do so he would need some help. He told me that if I worked hard, he would give me a piece of land. His father had left him some land and an old house. He never had any children of his own and had thought of me as a son. He told me that if I continued to work hard, go to school and open my own business that the land and house would be mine. So I did everything he asked me to. We helped each other out in those circumstances.

Without the help and guidance of the Mechanic, I wouldn't be who I am today. I grew into a young and successful man loving him as more than just my employer and mentor. I loved him as a father, just as he loved me like a son. Even though I hated my biological father, he was still my father. For that I took him under my wing and allowed him to live in that house with me.

My mother, God rest her soul, isn't on this earth anymore. She could only take so much stress when her body finally gave up. My father is now eighty-eight. As horrible of a father he was, he is a devoted grandfather now as my children absolutely adore him. I had met my wife as she would walk past the shop I worked at everyday on her way to school. Her parents thought I was a loser since I dropped out of school when I was twelve. She fought with her parents everyday about this as she was determined to be with me. My wife helped me to build my empire and gave me three beautiful children. I couldn't have accomplished what I did without her love and support. I love her more than I thought it was possible to love anyone. She, too, watches your show, better say, we watch it together.

Thank you once again for all that you do on "Your Life Experiences with Rah." Keep up the good work.

> *"Wow, I loved the happy ending of a husband and his wife. True love is so hard to find these days. It's sad to hear what a lot of women from earlier times went through with their husbands. when you hear these stories it makes you think: wow, she went through that? Can I handle that? may god bless her soul and may his mother rest in peace.*
>
> *This story also teaches us never to give up on yourself when the ones you look up to don't give you that support you need. Sometimes in the form of a stranger you will gain your praises. make sure to look out for it and don't dwell on looking for something that will never happen from the ones you want it to happen from. believe in yourself and praise yourself - as you alone can disappoint yourself and you alone can make yourself happy."*
>
> YLEWRAH

SUPERGIRL

Hey, Rah! I just want you to know how much I love the excitement of the segments that come on your show, dude! I hope that you share mine too and air it on Anonymous Monday's. My small family and I love your show and when we can't catch it live, we watch it on your YouTube channel. If you don't mind me asking, how did you come up with Your Life Experiences with Rah? I mean I understand why you are doing it and because of this show you are helping others. I guess my correct question is how did you make it a reality and air it every week?

I don't even know where to begin with my story. Shall I start with my parents falling in love when they were in college? Shall I start talking about the unconditional love my parents gave me? Or do I just say once upon a time and start the story like that? Why couldn't I just started off like this, my story is about a love triangle. There were three friends; two guys and a girl who loved each other equally. The problem was, it was time to get married which meant only two could stay and one had to leave. No one knew how to make this choice, so they all agreed to flip a coin to see which man stayed romantically in her life. That is how my parents became my parents. I didn't find out about this by finding old love letters or overhearing their conversations. You see, my parents were very open-minded and honest with me. I learned about their story through them, as odd as that might seem.

My father is mixed and was born in the United States. He comes from a Cherokee and Trinidad background, among other mixes. My mother was born in India. She has a Pakistan and Indian mix from her father and French, Italian and Canadian mix from her mother. When she got older, she moved to London. Eventually she moved to the US where she met my father and their friend. This explains where I got my beauty from and my gorgeous greenish blue eyes.

So back to the story, I'm sure you are wondering what happened to the other guy? Did he get his heart broken and commit suicide? Did he move to another state to get away from my parents? Do I know who he is? Well, we will just call him Uncle Sam which is short for Sameer and yes, we are keeping his identity anonymous. It is, however, a nickname that only my parents, him and I know about. Uncle Sam is a handsome guy with beautiful hazel eyes. His background is a mix of American and Pakistani. Before everyone jumps to the wrong conclusion, no, I am not his daughter. That is not what this story is about or so I thought.

My family is very small and we did have a few other blood relatives nearby. However, the person who was around us most of the time while I was growing up and spoiled me the most was Uncle Sam. He was there for every Thanksgiving, Christmas and other major holidays. We were his only family. His mother had died from cancer and a few years later his father had a major heart attack and passed away. My parents stood by him through all of his heartache. Uncle Sam is a stem cell regenerative doctor who had to travel for work to do research for a few years.

Even though the men flipped a coin to see who married my mother, they all kind of stayed as a couple. Whenever we would go on vacations, no matter how small the bed was I would find the three of them all snuggled up together. I grew up knowing the three of them as inseparable.

When he left to do his research, we all kept in touch with him thanks to technology. Sometimes we would visit him in different countries. Sometimes it would just be myself and my mother or myself and my father. At times I even went to visit him alone. When I was seventeen Uncle Sam was still away doing his research. We learned that he got really sick and thought he had some type of cancer. As sick as he was, he continued to do his research for another two years.

Rah, I love your drive after seeing your show on Wednesday and watching you for a few weeks after that. You do this show for others, but I think it is helping you as well. Keep up your energy and your drive and you will reach millions of hearts. By doing that, hopefully stories like mine will reach millions as well. Allowing people to not only appreciate love in every way but to comprehend that love has no boundaries. Our stories can help those that keep an open mind and are willing to learn that we are no longer living in the past where people condemn others.

My mother is a general surgeon at a well-known hospital where we live. It was my Mom's birthday and we all went out for this well-planned dinner with her work colleagues, other family members and of course Uncle Sam. This was the first time since Uncle Sam had come back from his job that he actually went out with us. That night he started coughing up blood and was rushed to the hospital. While he was there he found out that he needed a blood transfusion. I, the Supergirl, had blood type O negative which was what he needed. I was able to donate a pint. Rah, please encourage people to donate blood. It could save lives. What I noticed that night that I never saw while I was growing up was how much my parents truly loved Uncle Sam. They were both hugging and kissing him, while begging him not to leave them. Yes, my father was kissing him as well as my mother was. Reminiscing about this even though it has been years, still brings tears to my eyes.

Two days later after my Uncle was admitted, the doctors told us that he didn't have cancer. Rather he had a rare liver disease. He needed a transplant to have at least a fighting chance. We all went home that night and decided we would all go back to the hospital the next morning to get tested to see if we were a match for Sam. My only concern was that we weren't his blood relatives so the chances of us being a match weren't good. My mom reminded me that I was O negative and because of that I just might be a match. I looked at my parents and they had tears in their eyes and then looked at each other in the weirdest way ever. I was only nineteen at the time and was thinking I had my whole life ahead of me, so part of me selfishly didn't want to do this. Seeing the sadness and hope in my parents eyes, I couldn't say no. My parents did go on to tell me that if I was a match, I could still go on to live a healthy life after donating part of my liver. This is because the liver is the only organ that regenerates.

So I put my red cape on to be the Supergirl my family needed me to be and yes I was a match and on my way to save my uncle's life. The surgery went smoothly for the both of us. A couple of months later my uncle was living with us full-time. As I go on to type my story, a wave of emotion hits me. I will never forget the day I came home one evening. I opened the door to find a huge white polar teddy bear stuffed animal wearing a t-shirt that had a red heart with writing that said *thank you*. My mom walked over to me and hugged me. They were all grateful that I was my uncle's savior. She told me that my father was on the back terrace and wanted to talk with me. So I headed out back but saw my uncle there instead. I hugged him and asked him where my father was since he wanted to talk with me. He looked at me with tears in his eyes and I turned as I heard my mother saying to me that she told me my father wanted to speak with me. My father was holding my mother's hand at this point and had tears in his eyes as well. They walked towards my uncle. Rah, I suddenly became emotional not knowing why but knowing at the same time. My uncle walked over to me and took my hand and told me he was my biological father and hugged me. My mother and father embraced us in that hug as well. All three of them looked at me and told me it was true. I was in shock hearing this news. They were in the middle of explaining all of this to me and why they never told me the truth when I lost it! I pushed them away from me and told them they were all sick and sinners and ran into my room. They all ran after me and begged me to open the door. I was too upset and didn't open the door. So they started to explain all the why's outside of my bedroom door. They begged me once again to open the door as they wanted to sit down and discuss this as a family. So I took a deep breath and finally opened the door.

They told me how their love story began. They met in college. My mom was already dating my dad and very much in love with him when Sam came into their lives. Eventually they became a threesome. My mother never loved Sam the way she loved my dad, though. As their relationship progressed, they learned that my father could never get my mother pregnant. They learned this after my parents got married. Sam was able to give them something that my father couldn't. They always kept quiet about it and kept it as their secret to protect themselves and me as well. People are mean and that wouldn't have been a way for me to grow up, so they kept their secret from me as well. Something that still breaks my heart is when my dad thanked me for saving their Sam. I told them I would do it again and again. I do wish I had known the truth earlier but I honestly love all three of my parents equally. My Dad went on to tell me that they aren't gay. My dads have only been together with the presence of my mother and never with any other men. Just that their relationship works as a threesome instead of a twosome. They truly love one another and their relationship as well as mine with them blossoms throughout the years.

My message to everyone, listening to or watching your show, Rah, is to let everyone know that there is so much more that people share in their lives that we don't understand. So don't judge people. Don't hate people for doing something different. Don't condemn and stop living in the past. Live your lives to the extreme. Be happy always. My biological father, my Uncle Sam, is still alive and doing great thanks to my Supergirl powers. I was born in this wonderful world and because of that I was able to save a life. Nothing is more valuable than that.

"In this story, we learn that true love does exist. We learn that love and friendship are so great. We learn that hate has no part where love exists. We also learn that what's in the dark does come to light and what you hide has a way of showing its face. I love this story.

Let's focus more on friendship. Some people have friends in their lives and they just don't understand what that person will do for them and who they really are in their lives. a lot of people take the people in their lives for granted.

People need to learn to appreciate the people in their lives more and not to look for someone else to solve their problems — rather one should know they are there with you by your side as you go through your life challenges. Remember, it's no one's fault. it's not your friend's or family's challenge. it's all yours. you have to do what you need to do for you and remember "everything happens in the right moment."

YLEWRAH

SIDE CHICK

Rah, I really love watching Your Life Experiences with Rah. I think it is great that people have been able to share their stories to heal themselves and let others know that they aren't alone. Your show is not only inspirational, but it is also uplifting. I think about my story and the mistakes I have made. The biggest mistake I made was with a man whom I thought was my entire world. Choosing him over myself and my parents. Defying my parents for this man I loved. I wonder how I could have been so blind? I had taken my parents and their love for me for granted when this man came into my life. I was young and wild and didn't understand life till then. I thought my world began and ended with this man.

When I met this man, I thought that was it - that I didn't need to look for someone else now anymore. I believed he was my very own Prince Charming and we were going to live happily ever after. That is what you grow up thinking as a little girl - that one day your prince will come and throw you onto his horse while you ride into the sunset. My man had charm alright, but not like Prince Charming that you read about in fairytales. He had charm with his look and he knew how to work his words on me. I believed anything that he told me and that is what he wanted. Part of the charm in my eyes about him was that he was six years older than me. I couldn't believe he wanted to be with a girl like me or at my age. I fell and I fell hard and completely in love with this man. Nothing else in my life mattered so long as we were together.

You know they usually say a girl's first love is her father? I grew up thinking of my father as my hero. He was one of the good guys. Everyone adored my dad and said he was a godsend. Things change between daughters and fathers when another man enters the daughter's world.

That is what happened between my father and I. I betrayed and defied him in ways I am so ashamed about today. You see when I started dating this man I would get home very late, way past my curfew night after night. My dad wasn't happy with this situation so he grounded me and forbade me to see this man. Rather than accepting and obeying my father's wishes, I ran away. I was very heartless at that point in my life. All I left with was a note saying that I would be safe and that I needed to live my own life. I left and never turned back.

I found out a month later when I returned home that my father cried about my leaving every night. I know I could never rewind the clock and what is done is done but somehow I wish I could as my dad was a good man and didn't deserve a daughter like me. I thought karma would surely get me for what I did to my loving parents who didn't deserve what I did to them.

I was living with my boyfriend for a few weeks when this chick appeared. He told me it was just his cousin. It was a very strange situation as she was over at our place almost every night in the next months that would come. Of course, even though I had found their relationship strange, I never questioned it as they were family or so they told me.

About five years later I had gone on a vacation to California with my family for the summer. I ended up bonding with one of my cousins while we were there and opened up to her about my relationship. My cousin was very honest about her conclusion about my boyfriend. She felt that he was totally playing me. I didn't want to believe her, but what did she have to gain by lying to me? Therefore I did some investigating for myself and found out that he had cheated on me and has been lying to me for years. The guy I was madly in love with wasn't the man I thought he was. This man destroyed my life and I hurt my wonderful parents for him. He also tried to make me have his baby. Thankfully, I wasn't that type of girl who would just get pregnant so that Daddy stays by my side.

I had left him that day. It has been two and a half years since we had crossed paths. I was in school which was going great. I already had one degree under my belt. I was on a very progressive path to success in my life. He started to talk to me as just friends and my cousin warned me not to build anything with him again. I should've listened to my cousin as she had a clearer head than I did when it came to this man.

One night while I was asleep I got a phone call at 1 am in the morning that he was in jail. Apparently, he had an illegal business which I knew nothing about. The next few days I was just furious with all the countless lies and the fact that I once again fell for his charm only to find out there were more lies. Even though I was angry, I still did what I could to make his bail. That is when I learned that not only did he have an illegal business, but that he had put me at risk by exposing me to a life of crime without knowing it. I ended up failing all of my exams because of the emotional stress that man put me through.

Apparently, I was his side chick now. He had a girlfriend that knew about his illegal activities. She didn't care about that so long as she was taken care of financially and she could live a good life. Even after finding out about his illegal activities and his girlfriend, I still stayed with him. Fast forward to the time I came across his Instagram page and there were updated pictures of him and his so-called cousin. I noticed that she had posted a picture of her and her son. I also noticed how much her son looked like my man. Not only did he look like him, the age was coincidental as well. He was eleven. I confronted him about this and of course he lied to me. He could've lied to me until he was blue in the face and I still wouldn't believe him. There was no denying that the little boy was his.

I left him physically and emotionally that day. I went on Tinder and started to date. I ended up dating an ex-marine who is now a detective and I couldn't have asked for anyone better.

I hope my story reaches young girls and fathers. As a little girl we might know a little more and take our parents for granted. It is important to know that there are more important things in life than some man! Know that your parents will provide you with a better life than a man who allows you to disrespect and disown your own parents. Make sure to get an education so that you can stand on your own two feet with or without a man by your side. I hope my story can help others. That's why I shared it with you.

"She said it so nicely and as she said she hoped it reached others like herself. It's a bad thing when you have good parents and you define them or hurt them when you retaliate at times. There are some love stories you listen to as you hear how

the girl or guy goes against their parents for the person they love and it all ends well, but in this case you are doing this for a person who has no direction for himself in life. you have to know the direction you want in life from an early place at times. just like loving yourself when you speak to someone and they have similar directions as you, then you know somehow that person is also in a similar place and wants something good for themselves. Yes, I know at an early age we all tend to know more than we should and never listen — just remember without guidance we learn the hard way and have to handle the storms of life head on. mental health and stress hits you so hard then. we need to know we are able to handle all that life has to toss your way. see and think about the positives especially when others give us some good advice."

YLEWRAH

REAL NIGHTMARES

Rah, I just want to thank you for the great work you do on your show. My nightmare is one that played on repeat from the time I was a nine-year-old little girl and still goes on every night in my dreams. It started when my sixteen-year-old brother would come into my room after I fell asleep and rape me, night after night. He would make me do things to him and with him. Even though I knew what was going on was wrong I had to do it. If I didn't, he would've gone into my five-year-old little sister's bed and raped her even worse than he did to me. He threatened me with that and since I was only nine at the time, of course, I believed him. He had hurt me for days and I was in so much pain and wanted it to stop. As much as I wanted it to stop, I knew that if I did he would hurt my sister and it was my job to protect her. After all, I was the older sister.

When I fall asleep now, I think this night will be different. I will sleep well tonight. I will only have happy and peaceful dreams. I think this every night before I go to sleep and wake up every morning shaking because once again that horrible nightmare repeated in my sleep. My brother would hold my mouth with his big strong hands and would put his strong body over me so that I felt paralyzed because he held me down so hard that I couldn't move. Even though his hand covered my mouth I would scream as loud as I could, but no one ever heard me. He would hurt me so bad that I would pass out and wake up thinking it was over, only to realize he was still inside of me.

After a while of taking this torture, I decided to tell my mother. However, I had to be sure he wasn't doing this to my sister before I confided in her. So I questioned my sister for a few weeks to make sure my brother wasn't hurting her as well. I asked her if our brother ever tried to hurt her in any way? I would ask if he played rough with her at any time? She told me no - that he never hurt her. In fact, he rarely played or spent any time with her. Now that I knew she was safe, I could tell my mother what was happening.

I was finally ready to tell my mother what was going on so that my brother would stop raping me. At least I thought I was going to. However, the night I was going to tell her, she spoke first. She said she had a very disturbing conversation with my brother earlier. He told her that he had caught me watching him in the shower naked on more than one occasion. I felt like I just died, like there was no more hope. I couldn't breathe. I couldn't believe my mother believed my brother! She called me the Devil and Satan all in one sentence. I tried to tell her that he was lying but she kept on shaming me about being a sinner that is described in the Bible. She believed that Satan was drawing me into hell slowly. So she made arrangements with the pastor in our small town to pray for me but not in private. She wanted the whole church to know. She wanted to shame me in front of our entire community. So on that ominous Sunday, that is what happened. The pastor stood before everyone to cast the demon out of me while the real demon, my brother, sat in the congregation laughing at me. I felt lost. The woman who gave birth to me didn't believe me, not even the man who served God believed me.

When I was thirteen my brother started raping me during the day. It became easier since my parents were still at work and my baby sister who was now nine at the time was at her swimming lessons or ballet classes. One day he came home very angrily because his girlfriend who was a cheerleader had just dumped him and made a fool of him in front of all of his buddies. He saw me and slammed me against the wall and ripped off my clothes. Then he took out all of his anger and rage on me as he brutally raped me. When he was done I thought it was over but I was wrong. He pushed me down to the ground and tried to push his entire hand up my vagina; a new pain I had experienced that day.

I wonder how many people have nightmares of somebody on top of them and are fighting to get them off of them, but just can't? That fear in your sleep is so real that it wakes you up? You wake up and think it was just a dream even though it felt so real? I'm sure a lot of people do. For me it was different because I will hope and pray that it is just a horrible dream and will wake up and open my eyes and be safe. However, when I open my eyes, my nightmare is real. My brother once again was holding me down so hard that I couldn't move as he raped me. My own flesh and blood. My older brother. He was supposed to be the one I looked up to, my protector. Now he just became someone I feared. My brother destroyed me by what he did to me, both physically and mentally.

Fast forward to when I was in my twenties. I was on my way to celebrate a friend's twenty-sixth birthday. She only lived a few houses away from mine. She was too drunk to drive home, so I drove her car and took her home. Even though I only lived a few houses away, she handed me a small taser for safety. When I went to sleep, I tucked the taser under my pillow. When my brother entered my bed that night, I grabbed that taser and tasered that MOFO right in his testicles. That was the night I decided my brother would never hurt me again! He had fallen to the ground. He tried not to scream, but the loudness of the fall woke up my parents. They called out to see if I was ok? Believe it or not, I was still afraid that if I told them the truth my sister would pay the price so I said I had tripped and fell but that I was ok. Then I kicked my brother out of my room and warned him to never touch me again and that if he ever tried to touch our little sister that I would kill him! He never touched me again or went near our sister.

About three years later, it was my brother's wedding day. I didn't want to go but my parents forced me to. I was actually glad that they did because that was the day I met my husband. He was actually my brother's best friend and his best man.

It was supposed to be a happy day for my brother, after all it was his wedding day. Maybe it was his karma that finally got him? During the reception, a video played of his best man, my future husband and my brother's wife. It was the night before the wedding and the two of them were doing lines of cocaine by the pool which led to them kissing and doing things that weren't Christian. The pastor who was also watching this video, started to scream that it was Satan's work. Meanwhile, I thought it was an angel at work. My brother was livid watching this. Not only was he betrayed by his wife and best friend but he was humiliated in front of all of their friends and family. He had also been drinking all day as well as smoking pot and pushed his wife to the ground and stormed out! About five miles away he crashed into a lamppost that sent him into a coma. After two months of not being able to wake up, my parents decided to pull the plug.

My brother's best friend came by every day to see how I was doing during all of this. This is how we got close. After the funeral he told me that he blamed himself for my brother's death. I helped him get through his guilt and a year later we got married. Today we have two beautiful girls, ages six and eight. Not that it has been an easy marriage. As much as I know sex with my husband is supposed to be a beautiful thing between two people that love each other, I still struggle with that. After all my first sexual experience was anything but beautiful and it was with my brother. I grew up thinking sex was nothing but hatred.

The nightmares that replay in my sleep didn't help my marriage either. There was time after I woke up from a nightmare and I would jump out of bed and lock myself in the bathroom to splash my face with water. My legs would be shaking out of control. My husband would knock on the door and ask me what was wrong. I would lie and say I just had a nightmare. My nightmares would even happen while I was awake. My poor daughters saw me in a complete sweat while my legs and hands were shaking.

Years and years have gone by and I still have these nightmares which still feel like it is happening to me. I pray every night that they will go away. I went to therapy thinking that would help me, but it didn't. The one thing that does make it a little better is knowing he can't hurt me anymore because he is dead. Even though I know this when I'm awake, it is in my dreams that I don't. While I'm sleeping he is on top of me again and I can't move and I am so afraid to open my eyes. Maybe this will continue until I'm strong enough to tell my truth? Is it possible that by telling my truth I will gain my power back? Is that what it will take? Maybe? All I do know is that I have not mustered up my courage to tell my husband or my sister and eventually my daughters, I don't know if I ever will?

I share my story with you and your viewers to help others who have been in a similar situation. Maybe my story will help someone out there or maybe one of your viewers can help me get rid of my continuing nightmares? I don't know. What I do know is that talking and sharing is one step closer to gaining some peace.

"Just think about if the person you look up to is the one betraying you, taking advantage and dishonoring you by scaring you to have nightmares for life. your mother who should be protecting you and listening to you and believing you turns against you. This story will help millions. you all see how karma played off in this life changing story? sometime or the other whether you see it at that moment or sometime in life (but you will see it), when it does eventually come back, it will be worse than what you did to others.

Mental health is so strange when it hits and you just can't shake certain things. We do have to open our minds as we look towards the next day, which is our future. we can't hold on for too long onto the past. yes, it hurts, yes, it's what made you suffer and hurt. if it didn't happen you wouldn't be that strong person you are today and you wouldn't be able to help others as well. It's ok to let others know what you have been through as it helps. it's ok to let others know "it is going to be alright in the end".

YLEWRAH

MY WIFE AND BPD

Hey Rah, I am going to tell my story. I fell in love with and married a woman with borderline personality disorder. Of course, by the time I knew this was what was going on with her I was already in love. You know how the saying goes, but I love this person and therefore I will go to the end of the world for her.

The reason I want to share my story is because I love the mental videos on "Your Life Experiences with Rah." I must say, Rah, you are doing such a great job. People need to be aware of what goes on behind closed doors. There are so many different types of mental health behaviours that are triggered in different ways or from genetics. Not only is it hard for the person dealing with this, but for the people that come into his or her life as well.

She was my first love from high school. It was love at first sight, or so I thought. It was like we were the perfect couple. We did everything together and everything felt perfect. Things were going so well. We did everything right. We dated, got engaged and didn't live with each other until after our wedding. We got married so young, at twenty-three. It was then that the chaos began. Now that we were living together, she couldn't hide what was going on with her from me. Our marriage was in trouble. Somehow I got her to agree to go to marriage counseling. That's where I found out that she had been sexually abused by a family member when she was just a child. That apparently triggered her borderline personality disorder (BPD). My wife also confided in me at therapy that she had tried to go to therapy and go on medications before, but neither had worked. She was ashamed to tell me as she didn't want me to leave her.

I think about all the things that happened early on in our marriage and I wonder why I never saw this as a red flag. I guess it's true, love is blind? An instance happened six months after we got married. I thought it was great! I had a beautiful wife whom I was madly in love with and she even cooked for me. However, if I didn't get home from work in time when dinner was ready she would dispose of the food. When I would ask where the dinner was, that the house smells great, she would look at me and smile, then walk over to the garbage pail, open the lid and turn to me. Her smile would now change to a face of rage and say, "There is your damn dinner. Next time, come home on time!" Did I think this was odd? Of course, but we hadn't even been married a year yet. I thought we just have to get to know our schedules better and plan accordingly. I should've called her if I was running late.

A few months later I thought things were getting better as there hadn't been any more instances. However, something happened. This time it was worse than me just being late for dinner. It happened at work. My wife showed up unannounced at my office one day. It's a big office and therefore I had my own personal secretary. She noticed that my secretary was a lot prettier than I had led her to believe. So when I got home from work that evening she had a lot to say. She swore over and over that I was having an affair with my secretary and that is why I didn't tell her how pretty she was. Keep in mind that my secretary was two times my age. I thought my wife knew that I wasn't the type of man to cheat on her no matter what. I couldn't get over how much she was convinced that I was having an affair. It took me the whole night to calm her down and reassure her that she was the only woman I loved and cared for. Again, this should've been another sign that something was going on, but I loved my wife and didn't want to believe that anything was wrong with her.

As time went on more things would happen. Living with her became very stressful. I felt like at any moment she would explode if I said this or that. I felt like I had to tip toe in my own house. At times I would lose my patience and yell at her, forgetting how much I loved her. When that happened she would throw things and break some of our valuables just to get me angry. There was no excuse for some of her behavior, but then again she had been diagnosed with BPD in medical terms. This made it even more difficult because I knew she had a disorder and sometimes couldn't control the things she did.

A year and a half into our marriage our daughter arrived into the world. At the time I was working as well as studying medicine to become a doctor. I knew I needed to make a career change. I knew my daughter would be in trouble because mentally my wife couldn't parent our child. So I dropped out of medical school and became an accountant. I worked from home so that way if my daughter needed me I was there.

A few years later our son arrived. I wish I could tell you that the things were getting better, but that would be a lie. My wife acted very bipolar even though that is not what she was diagnosed with. BPD traits are very similar to bipolar. One moment she would be very social and friendly and then with a flip of a coin she would close down and not want anyone to be around her. She was very hostile with the kids, myself, her family and friends. At that point she was even threatening to hurt herself as a cry for help.

Rah, we could be having the best time with family and the kids. It would seem like a perfect day and then bam out of nowhere she would get very angry for no reason at all. It got so bad that she got upset about things the kids did months ago that had already been resolved. She would get all these horrible thoughts in her head about what would happen if I lost my job and how would we pay the mortgage? We would go to the theatre as a family to see a movie. In the middle of the movie surrounded by her family, she would just start to cry and scream out how lonely she was. Even though she started taking medication for her depression it didn't help her.

When my daughter was five and my son was eighteen months old I had gotten a promotion and a raise at work. I started working at a firm in an office setting once my daughter was old enough to attend nursery school. Naturally my wife thought the only possible reason for me getting those things was that I was having an affair. Mind you my boss was male and I was and am a straight man. Not only was my boss male, he was dying. He had been battling stage four skin cancer and passed away. May he rest in peace. The same day I got a promotion and a raise at work was the same day my wife threw me out of our home.

I moved in with my parents after my wife kicked me out of my own house. My wife lost it. She had called my family as well as her own and all of our friends to tell them what a horrible person I was because not only did I cheat on her, but I did it with a man and therefore I was a homosexual! She lost it even more when she had the nerve to tell my sweet baby girl who was only five that I was a penis sucker and that I was going to go to hell because of it.

I'm sure by now that anyone reading my story is pondering why I didn't leave my wife prior to her kicking me out. The thought never crossed my mind because we had two small children. I always believed that we would stick it out for our kids. I was wrong. On top of which, I was still very much in love with my wife. At the end of the day I couldn't leave my children; they needed me.

So back to my story. The day after she kicked me out of my house, I got word that she was at a bar with another man! It's a very small town and everyone knows and sees what is going on around them. Turns out that she had met this guy at a department store three months prior and had been talking ever since. So I finally put two and two together. My wife only accused me of having an affair because that was her way of getting me out of the house. She wanted me out of the house so that she would be free to date this man.

One of the traits of BPD is change. They want to change their last name, their hair color, even their job. People with BPD always feel underappreciated, so in order to feel any kind of value in the world is constant change. Change also means new excitement. So it's no surprise that she cheated. It was a change in her eyes, but it extremely hurt my heart as well as our children's.

I begged my wife to let me see my children for months before she finally agreed. Up till that point she made me out to be the enemy. She even had me questioning if it was my fault? I found myself apologizing to her! Even after all that happened, I was still in love with her and so of course I kept on apologizing. Truth is I was sorry. I wasn't sorry because I caused the problems and lies in my marriage, but because our marriage was over and I will always be sorry about that. I was also sorry for my children and that they had to experience all of this at such a young age.

About a year into my wife's new relationship things took a turn for the worse. This time it wasn't from her lies. That man brutally beat the crap out of her and then he just packed up and left her without saying goodbye or where he was going. Shortly after, my wife reached out to me but not to apologize for all the things she put me and the kids through. She wanted my sympathy as well as allowing me to let her back into my life.

This would continue to be a back and forth thing. I knew this wasn't healthy for the kids but I loved my wife. I also felt it was better if I lived under the same roof as my kids because I never knew if she was going to snap at the kids and I didn't want them to go through what I did with her.

For a brief time when my daughter was ten I was actually involved in a very healthy relationship. After my wife threatened to kill herself, I ended the relationship I was in and found myself once again apologizing. I apologized for allowing myself to experience a good and healthy relationship. My wife needed me and again I was worried about my kids living with her without me, so I went back.

I would like to tell you that my story got better and not worse. Unfortunately, I won't be able to do that. When my son was fifteen, he was diagnosed with borderline personality disorder. When I found this out, I didn't know what to do. So many thoughts ran through my head. I had now been living with this for years with his mother. I understood a lot of it. She couldn't control the things she did or thought, but I didn't want that life for my son or anyone that came into his life. It was heartbreaking to see it happening to my wife and now I would have to watch my son going through it. I didn't know how to react or what to say to him to make him feel better about his diagnosis. I did, however, make sure to tell him how proud I was of him each and every single day. I even blamed my wife, because my son wouldn't have this disorder if it wasn't for her. I knew I was wrong to think that, but I'm an honest person and that thought did go through my mind. My wife was always hard on our son which didn't help his BPD. At age nineteen our son committed suicide.

I was an emotional mess after losing my son but I continued to stay with my wife for an additional five years before I had enough. I had to make sure I was there for my daughter. I couldn't bear to lose another child. I made sure my daughter knew how much she was loved and that I won't leave her.

Staying with my wife came with emotional as well as financial losses. She was once again cheating on me with a young man in his twenties. She took him to Las Vegas, but not before she withdrew all of our savings. Eighty-five thousand to be exact! She even took a loan out against our house and spent that money as well on this man who was just using her. I'm fifty-four now and I ponder if I will find a woman who will appreciate me as a man? Will I be able to love again? Do I even know how to love? I question everything because I had to in my marriage. I would like to think I will fall in love again and this time it will be pure love. A love where we can both count on each other. A love where there is trust, communication and laughter, a lot of laughter. I hope so. I wish for it every night.

My advice to all of you reading my story is this: life is too short to settle for anything that isn't pure happiness. Notice the red flags. Leaving someone who isn't mentally stable does not make you a bad person. I love my children and for that I have no regrets, even though it was a very hard life. I think a lot of times about how I knew my wife wasn't mentally stable and yet I still had two children with her. We are human and when we are in love, we want that love to grow through children. We think maybe having children will make things better. Love is blind and makes us do things without thinking. So take your time in a new relationship. You have to remember that you, too, are important and you deserve to be happy.

"I ask this to myself all the time: "Would I stay with someone I know who is mentally ill, sacrificing my happiness and peace of mind? or would i let this person go out there and destroy another human being, sending them into the same depressed state they have put me into?" Some are really built to take a lot of mental pressure while others are not. I think I do it because I love helping until I can't anymore. I know many people are like this in this world. and i must say hats off to this amazing human being who has endured so much even losing his own kid. Sometimes you take a lot upon yourself like it's your responsibility to save that person or be the right person in their life but you have no one to pull you up while you are sinking deep in the darkest places of life. you have to always keep in mind what you can mentally handle. I know millions can relate to this story and millions have been in a place where they know that enough is enough and know you have given it your best try before walking in the opposite direction. "remember you can only handle to a certain extent."

YLEWRAH

MY STEPFATHER, THE BEAST

Hello my friend, I just want to tell you how much I appreciate you and what you do on "Your Life Experiences with Rah." I am also a gay Caribbean man. I was born in Jamaica and now live in Detroit. The stories that jolted my heart were "My Father Made Me His Wife", the one with the woman who stripped naked and then walked through the streets of Guyana and "Fat Sweet Bottom". After hearing those stories, I decided to share my story with you and to all of your viewers. Maybe someone else out there went through a similar situation or is now and by hearing my story it will help them to know they are not alone.

When I was only four years old my father was shot and killed. I barely remember him as he died when I was very young. Not too long after my father passed, my mother met another man and ended up marrying him. Shortly after they were married my sister entered the world. I thought everything was going to be fine. My mom was happy again and I had a new baby sister but there were things going on that I didn't understand yet as I was only six years old. I had seen Cinderella at that point but never did I think I would be living her story.

I remember the first time my step-father laid eyes on me, he hated me. I never knew why he hated me. After all, I was just a small child. Maybe it was because I wasn't his child and It was a constant reminder to my father. I grew up so fast that I didn't even get to enjoy my childhood. Like I said I was only six and already I was taking care of my baby sister, cleaning, cooking and even doing laundry. Yet, my step-father was never pleased with what I did.

My mother was the breadwinner in their marriage. My stepfather didn't contribute. He would stay home and play cards all day and do drugs and then he even started to sell them. Not that he financially contributed from the money he got from selling drugs. He used that money to buy more drugs. I started to refer to him as "The Beast" after he started to brutally beat my mother. It wasn't like my mother could even afford to stay home as she was the only one working. So no matter how badly she was injured, she would still go to work.

My stepfather was six feet tall and his eyes always looked bloodshot red. I used to think it was because he had Satan's eyes, but now I realize it was from him smoking pot. I was convinced he was the devil!

Three years later I was nine. I had the flu but that didn't matter to "The Beast". He needed me to get him alcohol at his friend's store and he didn't care that I was sick. All he cared about was getting the liquor so he just ordered me to go. When I got back I was shivering and had a really high fever. I thought he was going to tuck me into bed and apologize for sending me outside when I was so sick. Instead, my worst nightmare happened. He told me he had something that would make me feel a lot better. So I looked at him to see what he was going to give me and I saw him pulling down his pants. I was so confused, I didn't know what to do so I just froze. He made me watch him please himself and then told me to sit up and open my mouth. I was still so confused and shocked at what was happening. So as I sat up and opened my mouth, I closed my eyes as he came closer to me and then I felt a thick fluid fill my throat. What did I just swallow? Did that just come from my stepfather's penis? Is that what happens when you touch yourself? You have to understand I was only nine and while I had suspicions of what it means to masturbate, I still didn't know for sure yet. He made me believe that he was helping me. That his fluids that just entered my mouth and was forced to swallow was medicine to help me feel better. However, as I was swallowing this I started to vomit. He slapped me and grabbed me by my neck calling me a batty boy (Jamaican swear word for gay) and made sure I swallowed. He then went on to tell me that if I told my mother that he would beat her so hard that he would kill her!

Surprisingly enough that was the last time he did that to me. That was until five years later when I was fourteen. My mother had gotten a new job in the city and she moved there with my sister and only came home on the weekends. As time passed, she came home less and less. I didn't want to move away from my friends so I stayed with my stepfather.

One afternoon after I got home from high school my stepfather was home with a couple of his friends smoking pot and drinking. I knew not to bother him when he was in that state so I just started doing my chores. We didn't have any running water to shower or wash dishes with. I had to fill barrels of water from the stand pipes that were a few houses away from us. This was part of my daily routine. Once I got the water I took a shower. While I was in the shower, I heard a very loud banging noise. I got out of the shower to open the bathroom door and there he was again, a man I hadn't seen in years. "The Beast" was back. He pushed me down onto the toilet with my butt in the air. I started to cry now that I was old enough to realize what was going to happen. I begged for him to stop but he didn't. I couldn't see anything as he was holding my head down with one hand. He was rubbing my bottom with his other hand and then I felt one finger slip into my butt and then two and three fingers were up there. At first he was slow and gentle but I guess he was quickly aroused because he started to get aggressive. Then there was a different sensation and this one really hurt. I suddenly felt a sharp pain and it felt like it was ripping up my insides. That lasted for about fifteen minutes and yet it felt like hours to me. When he was done he spit on my butt and called me a batty boy before leaving the bathroom. I was left in my own pool of blood. I never experienced pain like that before. I was in so much pain and after looking at all of the blood I passed out. I experienced severe cramping for about three days after that. I thought each time I went to the bathroom I had diarrhea, at least that's what it felt like. However, when I wiped myself, I saw that it was blood.

He raped me once more before my mother came home for the weekend. I had heard them talking about me but I didn't think he was confiding in her about what he did to me. After all he had told me not to ever tell anyone, otherwise he would kill my mother. He must have told her I did something to him because when my mother saw me she didn't hug me. Rather, she banged my head on the stove so hard that I fell to the ground. While I was on the ground, she hit me with a piece of wood telling me that "The Beast" was her man and that I couldn't have him. She also said while she was beating me that she didn't raise a batty boy. I couldn't believe my mother believed these lies. The man that beat her time after time again and yet she took his word. I was so heartbroken. How could a woman who gave birth to me believe such lies about her own child?

I never confronted my stepfather, as I didn't want to provoke him to rape me again. Things once again got quiet for a few months. My uncle, who is my dad's brother and his family came for a visit from the USA. I went to stay with them for a few days. My cousin who was seventeen was innocently playing with me. We had always been close so I'm not sure why I suddenly became afraid? I wanted to tell him what happened but I was afraid for my mother and honestly, I was ashamed that I allowed it to happen. He had sensed that something horrible happened to me and after a few days he convinced me to open up to him. After I did, he told me that he had to tell his parents what was going on and that I couldn't go back to live with "The Beast". My aunt said she had to get permission from my mother before I could live with her and her family. I now had hope. It was small, but finally I had some hope.

Well that hope faded fast. It was now a month prior to my sixteenth birthday and I was ordered by "The Beast" to make a pot of beef stew and to bring it to his friend's house for his birthday. When I arrived there were three of his friends already getting high and playing dominoes for money. I left the pot of stew on the stove and made my way to the door to leave and head back to home. However, "The Beast" cornered me and told me that I wasn't allowed to leave. He said that it was his friend's birthday and that I needed to show him a good time. His friend then came into the room and offered me a drink. Mind you I was still a minor and I didn't taste any liquor yet at this point. So I kindly declined and again tried to leave. Both he and my stepfather said I was being rude and disrespectful by not having just one drink to toast for his birthday. His friend said if I just had one drink with him for his birthday he would allow me to go home. They were drinking Jamaican Rum which is very strong. I wasn't allowed to sip it because they poured it into a shot glass and told me I had to do it in one shot! Man, I felt like my chest and throat were on fire! A few minutes had passed and now the room was spinning. So they had me sit down on the couch. Five minutes later they handed me another shot.

I had thought ok they got me to take a few shots and now they would let me leave? I was getting up to do just that when another friend came over to me with a joint and told me to take a hit. I glanced over to see my stepfather who had that look on face that if I declined I would end up paying the price for it. So I gave in and smoked the joint. Now the room was really spinning! Another shot glass was given to me. I attempted to drink it but as it was going down, I spit some of it out. My stepfather was not happy seeing this and came over and slapped me hard against my face. At the same time he was calling me all these nasty things. His friends came over to stop him and ask him what was wrong with him, why was he hitting me? My stepfather's best friend, the one who was having the birthday celebration came over to me to tell me not to worry and to go lie down in his bed and rest up. I wanted to just go home but he told me I wasn't in any position to go home. He told me to go to his room and lie down till everything stops spinning. When I finally agreed and got into his bed he told me not to worry. He told me I would no longer feel any pain. It was a blur but I remember seeing him walk over to his dresser and pull something that I couldn't make out of his draw. All of the sudden I felt a sharp needle go into my arm and then I blacked out.

When I regained consciousness, it was still a blur. I remember seeing about ten men around me that were naked and laughing. When I was blacked out, someone had turned me over so that I was laying face down on the bed. One by one they raped me and each time I once again felt that sharp pain that traveled from my back into my stomach and then I passed out. It took my body days to recover from being repeatedly attacked. That horrible attack haunts me till this day no matter how much I try not to remember it.

When I woke up this time there was a man I hadn't seen earlier. Even though I was very weak I managed to get myself up and off of that bed. I was trying to get out of that room before the man saw me because I didn't know if he now was going to rape me or not. I tried to tip toe out of the room but he caught my eye. As he did he said, "Oh good, you are up." He advised me to shower because I smelled. I froze and just started to cry as all the pain started to flood me again. I looked down and saw dried blood on my legs. The man got up and said I can't leave without taking a shower first. He then led me to the restroom. When I got out of the shower, he had asked me if I was hungry or if I needed anything. All I wanted was to leave and never come back.

As I was heading home, I feared what would happen when I got there? As I was walking I noticed an old woman carrying some bags. She looked up and asked me to please help her. Somehow helping that lady made me forget all the pain I was in. Before I left her, she turned to me and said, " I want you to know that your current journey will end soon and a new life will begin." She also wanted me to know all that has been going on since my mother got remarried was none of my fault. Who was this lady? How did she know what was going on in my life? Was she an angel? I'll never know.

As I got closer to home I noticed there was a car parked in the yard. When I got inside of my house my mother was there with my aunt, uncle and my cousin. My mother turned to me to tell me I could go with them and live in America. We left that night. My mother hugged me tight and told me not to forget her before she finally released me.

Twelve years after living in Detroit my mother came to visit me. I had a long heart to heart talks with her and told her the truth about her husband and the horrible things he put me through. This time she believed every word from my mouth. She apologized for not being there for me when I had needed her the most.

My sister, the healthy one, married a very rich young man who treated her like she was a treasure. They had two sons together. Her eldest son was gay. I had finally gotten up the courage to tell my sister about her father. Not because I wanted to destroy her image of him, but because I wanted her to understand why there was such a distance between us. I didn't want her to think any less of me and that I was scared that he could've easily done all those horrible things to her had she come back home. She was livid and hurt that not only did I go through that but that I had to endure it on my own. She was also very mad and hurt that her own father could do such awful things. Her father was found dead from an overdose a few months after I told her my story.

My aunt passed away three years ago from cancer. My uncle is still alive. He is old now but still the loving man I always knew him as. My cousin got married and had three beautiful children. Sadly one of his children died at a young age from heart disease.

It took me a very long time to believe there were good men in the world too. I met a man in my late thirties. We were together for eight years before we got married. Unfortunately in 2015 he was diagnosed with a rare disease and he died. It was a short time that I had with my husband, but it was time that I will always treasure. Time I thought I would never experience.

Just know that even if you are living in the storms, it eventually has to pass and when it does the sun will shine through. When that sun does come out, do everything possible to soak it in.

> *"This is not just courage, but you are a hero in my eyes. any of you reading this and falling into any part of this wonderful soul's life story, i want you to give yourself a pat on your back and let you know how amazing you are and tell "you" thank you for bringing yourself this far. Every time I read this story, I cry and I feel this child's pain. i see evil - i see the evil that is a true horror story. demons that you make into something so beautiful for a horror movie or novel and sell to scare others are something out of art and imagination, but these men are what you call evil. I know there are millions out there in a similar story of rape and molestation, even prostituted at young ages. my love goes out to all as I know that one day it will be over soon. any of you reading this and going through something or knows someone going through something similar, please know and let them know to "believe that it will all come to an end soon. It will be over soon."*
>
> YLEWRAH

MY MOTHER STOLE HER MOTHER'S HUSBAND

I am sixty-two years old now and thanks to my husband, children and grandchildren I have learned so much about what life actually is. Also, thanks to you and your show "Your Life Experiences with Rah," that I have also learned about life and started appreciating gay people. I am from Trinidad and have been watching your show for a month now. Your show is very interesting and I have seen a few stories that were very melancholic. My story is similar to the one where the guy said his mother was deceitful. My mother was no different from his. As you read my story you will get to know the truth. Rah, you are right that God never teaches anyone to hate anyone. God is love and created all of us out of love and to only have love in our hearts. In the beginning of my life I didn't believe in God. I started to believe when I begged God to save me and my son when we both got very sick. I saw his grace in doing so and believed ever since.

So a little bit about my past. My grandmother's (from my maternal side) first husband died. Before his death, they had a daughter who is my mother. After my grandmother's husband passed, she remarried when my mother was thirteen. Through my grandmother's second marriage she gave birth to three sons. My grandmother and her new husband used to work in the fields as my mother told me. My mother said from the time she saw her stepfather, she knew she liked him. My mother told me that my grandmother was a bitch and didn't appreciate her husband. That she would push him around, especially when he came home after a night of drinking.

My grandmother had gone over to her brother's house one evening to take care of him since he had been sick when my mother was fifteen years old. My grandmother had told my mother not to worry. That her stepfather would come home drunk and not even realize that she had been out. So she told my mother to just tell him when he wakes up in the morning where she was and why and that she would be back by lunchtime.

My mother used this opportunity to make a move on her stepfather. So that evening rather than going to bed in her own room, she went to sleep in her mother and stepfather's room. She was very smart. She knew her stepfather would come home drunk and would attempt to turn the light on by the bed, so she moved it to a place he wouldn't be able to get to. As she thought, when he came home he was very drunk. He took off all of his clothes and got into bed thinking he was lying next to his wife, not his stepdaughter! Of course my mother didn't tell him it was her and she allowed him to have his way with her that night. He was in fact surprised to see her sleeping beside him when he woke up the next morning. My mother completely lied to him. She told him that she was scared to fall asleep in her bed alone and so she went into her parents room. She went on to tell him that he came home very drunk and raped her before he passed out. He was horrified and begged my mother to keep this secret between them and that he would do anything she wanted so long as she didn't tell anyone.

A few weeks later my mother found out she was pregnant as a result of the rape as she told him. She told her stepfather that he had to leave her mother and marry her so that they could raise the baby together. As you must've put two and two together by now, my mother's stepfather is my biological father; my grandmother's second husband. Crazy, right?

My father has now passed away. When he was alive, I always wondered what my mother had on that man? She stole my father from her own mother! She never even looked back, not even when my grandmother passed away.

I never got the love of a father growing up. Anytime I tried to get close to my father my mother would beat me and accuse me of wanting her man. I never understood why until I learned about her story. My mother was very abusive to my father as well. Even with all the abuse she still had four more children with him. When I was fourteen I ran away and went to live with my uncle who was my mother's brother. I thought I had gotten myself into a better living situation. However, one night while I was asleep I woke up to my uncle's brother-in-law on top of me. I jumped up and tried to get out of his hold. He wouldn't let me go. Instead, he pulled my head down onto the bed and took two of his fingers and put them inside of me. He wasn't gentle and the pain was so horrible. I thought he was going to do more to me but that was all he did. I'm not sure why he stopped, but I was glad that he did. When I woke up the next morning I decided to go back home.

When I got home my mother gave me a good beating for running away. After what happened at my uncle's, I decided it was better to get beaten up by my mother rather than being raped by a monster. I never told my mother about what almost happened when I stayed at my uncle's home. I knew she wouldn't have believed me or would've told me I had done something to turn him on and then beat me for it.

The years seemed like forever. I would go to work with my mother. She had a mini market shop in our village. When I was sixteen I met my first husband who was five years older than me. He would come to the shop when my mother wasn't around and we would talk and get to know one another. A few weeks later he asked my mother for my hand in marriage. I guess it was her way of getting rid of me and so she gave us her blessing.

I thought I was going to finally experience what having a good life was. In the beginning of our marriage, it was just that. My husband's parents gave him land to build a house on. He was so loving to me during this time. After we got settled into our new home my husband got a job with his cousin in the West. There was a time when he didn't even come home, especially on the weekends. He also started to drink very heavily. By the time I was nineteen I had three small children that I was left to raise on my own since my husband was rarely home. That is also when my in-laws moved in to help me with the kids since their son was hardly home.

Sporadically, my husband would come home to give me money and have his way with me before he went on the road again. When I was twenty and my eldest daughter was four, my parents came over for a visit. They had brought vegetables and other things for us. That evening my husband came home and saw all that my parents did for us. Rather than being grateful, he got very angry and beat me. As he did he yelled that he was the man of the house and he doesn't need my parents thinking that he isn't. My husband's parents lived with us. They were only forty feet away and heard what their son was doing to me and did nothing to stop it.

During that beating I knew I was pregnant again. I was going to tell him that I had missed my period, but he was too busy hitting me and making sure I knew he was the man of the house. Unfortunately, I never got to tell him that I was pregnant. That beating led to miscarriage.

Fast forward a little bit to why I started working. My husband was rarely home and when he was to drop off money it wasn't enough to support myself and three young children. So I decided it was time for me to make some of my own money. A friend of mine had an aunt who had a big cleaning business. So she would always line me up with cleaning jobs that paid well. This wonderful lady had a very handsome younger brother who was around my husband's age. He liked me a lot and knew that I had three children and issues with my husband. One day I saw him leaving my house after speaking with my in-laws. He went to ask for their permission to marry me. Even though my husband abandoned me and my kids, I was still legally married to him and so how could I marry someone else?

About a month later my husband came home. When he did, his father went to talk with him about his disappearance. My husband was furious that his father dared to speak to him about his marriage. He got so angry that he picked up the shovel next to him. He was about to hit his father with it when my brother-in-law luckily saw this and grabbed the shovel out of his brother's hand. He was still angry. He pushed his kids out of his way and then grabbed me. He took off his belt and beat me with it. My five-year-old daughter was hysterical as she watched her father hurt her mother like this. She ran over to cover me and as she did, the belt whipped her. My husband didn't even realize his daughter was covering me. Just as he was about to whip me with the belt again, my daughter screamed. He saw her face and realized what he did and just ran out of the house.

That day when he ran out mortified at what he had done, he was run over by a truck that killed him. His cousin came to see me later that month. My husband had a lot of money that he had compensated through the company he had worked for and his cousin came to bring that money for me and the kids.

About a month had passed. I was just getting home from work and picking up the kids from school. My in-laws called me over to talk with me. When I got into the living room, a little boy about two and a half years old was sitting beside them. They told me that a few hours ago a woman had knocked on their door to tell them this was their grandson and now that their son was gone she didn't have any way of supporting the child. So she left him with his grandparents and left.

I took in that little boy and loved him as if he was one of my own. Now that I was free from my marriage, I ended up marrying the other guy and we had two beautiful children together. My new husband and his family were devotees of Goddess Durga and I personally think she called me as my struggle didn't just end there.

My husband and I opened a clothing store and a supermarket. He was really my angel sent by Devi Durga. My problems were no longer physical abuse; they were now health issues. My youngest son had gotten very sick with a strange disease. From the stress of him being so sick, I got sick too. Like I said earlier in my story, this is when I started to believe in God. This is why my son and I survived that illness.

An update on my mother, father and little sister. My sister unfortunately went through a bit of hell with our mother as well. When she was sixteen she had gotten her heart broken. My father was hugging her and telling her that she would be ok when my mother walked in and saw that and lost it. My mother pulled my sister out of my father's embrace and slapped her! My father picked up his walking stick and beat my mother with it. After that, my mother never abused her or our father again.

My father died a few years ago. That is when my mother told me and my sister about her story and how my step-grandfather became my father. I looked at her and told her that she would suffer for what she did to him. She went on to tell us that she and our father were slaves to our grandmother and needed a way out. So that was why she did what she did. My mother is now seventy-eight and stronger than ever. Maybe after saying aloud what she did she realized how wrong and crazy it was. Or maybe it was from my father's beating that made her see her ways. Whatever it was, she had finally changed and for the better. She turned into the mother I wished I had when I was a little girl. So, you see it is never too late to turn your life around.

Thank you, Rah, for allowing me to share my story with you. You are a really sweet and handsome guy. Bless your mother for bringing you into this world. I will pray that Devi Durga will bless you as I know her miracles are real.

"This is part one of this story. After speaking to her, she sent me the other part of the story. Please see the next story."

TO BELIEVE IN SOMETHING YOU NEVER KNEW ABOUT

One day my son woke up with a very high fever. On taking him to the doctor, he said it was just the flu. After a few days, the fever was not going down and so I took him to the doctor, who sent us to the hospital. By the second week of testing, not finding what was causing this infection or where it was coming from made him turn pale at times. I started to get this unbearable pain in my stomach.

They finally said he had some periodic fever and other things they started treatment for at that time. They even said stuff about organ inflation. The week before that, next to my son was a little girl. One day her grandmother came to visit her. She later informed me she had to remove her appendix. When I saw her placing a red flower by the little girl's head, what caught my attention.

Hello, can you explain to me why you did that? And she started off without any hesitation with so much belief and faith in what she did. "This Flower was sent by the Devi to get her well." As she continued," don't be disheartened or scared. I am a Goddess Durga's devotee; before I left the house, I went to pray to Devi Durga Maa. I am not sure of your religion. Still, Maa Durga won't care about religion. She looks at everyone as her children. She looks at you as her child. When a child cries to a mother and how you as a mother react that's how Durga Devi acts for her children. She said to me before she could walk away after finishing her prayers for her granddaughter, this flower fell to her feet, and all she heard was a voice that said the word head. She went on to tell me, "Now, my child, if I tell you where that flower was, it's another story. You seem like you need a miracle as well let's share this flower" she took that flower break it in half, placing half by her granddaughter and the other half by my son head "looking at my son she said oh he is a very handsome little guy he has to grow up to have at least 4 children he's a fighter you could never tell he might be able to help little kids like himself someday."

Tears came out of my eyes. I sat down and cried and told her everything that's been happening, telling her I only pray because my husband and his family do it. She said, "go to Durga and consider her a mother, the type of mother that you are, and she will help you the same way you will help your kids think of her as the mother you always wanted." As she walked, kissed her granddaughter, and left the room, I broke down. She knew nothing about me. How could she know I never had a good mother? I hugged my son, and I started to beg Devi Durga to save my son.

After an entire week, my son was out of the hospital. As he came home, I went to where my husband prayed, taking a picture of Devi Durga dropping to the ground on my knees, bawling out to her "thank you, Maa" thank you for expressing that she is my actual mother, telling her don't ever leave me alone in the world again.

I went to numerous doctors who said I had an ulcer to find out some of my organs moved up into my diaphragm. I learned that happened from all the beatings I got from my husband and mother. I prayed to Durga Devi until the doctor found a lump in my breast but sent me to another doctor to double-check. During this time, Hindus prayed to Devi Durga in her other forms.

(Hindus call this festival "navratri," the workshop of the different forms of Devi Durga Maa, who is the goddess of everything and the universe know her also as "the universal mother" just as we all play a part in life; hence in hinduism, Maa Durga took on different forms for different jobs as we have in this human life. The job of a doctor, a lawyer, a teacher, an engineer, a cook, etc and most importantly, she never stops being a mother to all who loves her and believes in her)

My mother-in-law prayed to Devi Durga. After it was finished, there were particular offerings for the Devi, which I learned was her favorite offering. I sat in front of the Devi, admiring her to tell her mother that you changed my life and gave me happiness. All I ever wanted was to see my children growing up and be happy before I leave and see my husband be happy with his children's success. All I heard was "eat me," and I looked down, and this particular offering was glowing. Like a bright light was coming from it. I immediately remembered the flower falling on that grandmother's foot without thinking. I picked it up, sat, and ate it. Told my husband what had happened, and he smiled, saying she wanted you to have it to cure you.

Next week the new doctor informed me that there wasn't any lump. All the rest of the complications I had all vanished. I don't have any health issues, no BP, no diabetes. All thanks to Devi Durga. I never practise as a Hindu, but the bond I have for the Devi will never change. Over the years, people told me when I get something, the Devi will take something I must give her a coconut. One thing when I do something for my children, if they were to ask or not, is I don't wish for anything in return their love and goodness of making me proud is all I wanted, and that's how I felt Devi Durga was in my life she was my mother and would think like me, so I never had to do anything in the return of her love. Mostly I would buy her a bouquet of flowers once every so often and say, Maa, thank you. I would hold that picture, kiss her, and tell her I love you, MAA.

Rah, if people were to sit and listen to those stories you have been sharing, many people's lives will change "if they listen." If those people hear the words you use, especially "believe" and "love," they will elevate to different levels on whichever dream they would pursue, giving their life a complete balance of peace, love, happiness, and bliss. All they all have to do is, as you say, "believe and love themselves." Great job, rah I'm proud of you.

"we hear stories about people like her mother all the time in so many ways. some of you reading this don't even realize you might be this same "woman/man" who stole her own mother's husband. don't be mistaken, let's put ourselves in her mother's shoes. she did whatever she thought was right to make her happy. most of you do that, and those things unknowingly with ambition could destroy and put another person into a terrible mental place. now put yourself where it is. you are in a horrible mental and toxic place and atmosphere. you have

the complete right to look for that beaming light shining it's way inside and to go after it as long it makes you happy and sane in the end, giving you that inner peace knowing you didn't do anything wrong. but looking out for your well-being and happiness and maybe returning a little bit of that mental stress or ten times the stress they were putting you through isn't so bad after all?

"As for this unique soul? Wow, hats off to her and how she dealt with her struggles. You who are reading this, did you ask yourself: "did she go through all that?' It's hard at times when we hear someone's story, and our heart breaks for them. our tears flow like in her story. I assure you she could have handled it just like planned, and she did. She is a woman who has taken life and given life the ride of its own because she rode the waves of those tsunamis like a professional who knew that one day it would all end. I wish people would understand some stories like hers and understand that today's problem will be over soon. before we couldn't tell what the build-up would be like. We didn't know how many more challenges we would have to face while finishing off another project. She handled life very well. I want you all to know this and know that life will kick you to the ground. you may have heard this a million times, but you need to visualize the sky, and that's where you need to reach for. look at the stars and the moon, and keep grabbing for them when you are on the ground. you will definitely find yourself when you see yourself so far from the ground you were once on. Keep believing in yourself. rah loves you and believes in you."

YLEWRAH

MY FATHER

We were a family of four living in Trinidad. It was me, my older sister and my parents. I remember that people used to say that my sister and I were born with a golden spoon. I don't know about that. I was young at the time, so what did I know?

What I do recall is how my parents raised me and my sister. They taught us discipline and responsibility. They taught us how important education is. My parents had a business in Trinidad where we had resided. We were Hindus and very religious. My father did everything by the books. He fasted when he was supposed to, he prayed every morning and evening. He was also the perfect husband and father. My mother was the kindest person with the warmest of hearts. She wore her heart on her sleeve. She would help anyone in need, including strangers. The one thing that she loved more than her own life was my father. I would hear her tell my sister on more than one occasion that once she married, her husband would and should always come first before anyone.

Rah, I have watched Your Life Experiences with Rah more than once. You speak about karma and how sometimes we have to pay for something we did in a previous life. As a Hindu I have heard that saying over and over, "God is testing your faith." My question to you is who do we blame when bad things happen to good people?

My mother was the one responsible for cashing out the drawer at the end of each business day. She would leave a hundred dollars in the drawer every evening so that there would be money for change on the next business day and bring the earnings of the day upstairs to put into the safe. One Sunday afternoon as she was coming back down to lock up the store, a woman and three men walked in. My mother went to greet them as the men pulled out guns aiming them at her and ordered her to give them all of the money. So my mother went and opened the cash register and handed the men the hundred dollars that was in the drawer.

The men weren't happy about the little amount of money that was handed to them. They got very angry and started to smash things. I guess the woman with the men got afraid as she ran out of the store once the men started to break things. My father heard all this noise and ran downstairs to see what was going on. The men saw my father and pointed their guns towards my mother. They told my father that they would shoot her if he didn't get the rest of the money that should've been in the drawer.

My sister and I entered the store not knowing what was going on. When we tried to make a run for it, one of the men grabbed my sister by the neck and threw her to the ground. At that time my father came downstairs with the remainder of the money and saw my sister on the ground with guns pointed at her. The men took the money and then ordered my mother to go upstairs and collect all of the jewelry or they would kill her daughter.

While my mother was collecting the jewelry the rest of us were held at gunpoint and directed upstairs to our living room. They made us all lay on the floor face down. When my mother came into the living room with the jewelry, she was told to get onto the floor face down near my father. My parents begged the men not to hurt us, after all we gave them all of our money and all of our jewelry. One of the men came over to my mother and put his gun into her mouth. He told her that if she opened her mouth again that he would kill her family one by one.

I was only fourteen when this happened and my sister was sixteen. While one man had a gun to my mother, the other made my sister stand up so that he could look at her. She glanced at her for a few moments and then started to put his hand on her and grabbed her bottom. My father looked up and saw this and he screamed. He begged them to take whatever they wanted as long as they didn't hurt his wife or children. Both men wanted to shut him up so they went over and as one kicked him in his back, the other turned him around and kicked him in his stomach. Then they stopped and asked him if he was jealous that they were touching his daughter and not him? So they bent down and pulled his pants down to his knees and flipped him over onto his stomach again as one of the men slid his gun into his butt. When my mother saw this she couldn't help it and screamed! She was yelling out, "Please stop, please leave us alone, please do not hurt us." One of the men walked over to her and grabbed her and pulled her up off of the floor with her hair. He then told her that she doesn't learn, grabbed her neck, held it back and put his gun down her throat and said, "now you will shut up!"

Then when I thought things couldn't get any worse, it did. The men grabbed my mother and my sister and raped them, each having their way with them. They had tied up my father so that he could watch as each man had his way with his wife and his daughter. He would see the fear in their eyes and hear how afraid they were by their screams, yet he was tied up and couldn't do anything but watch. There is nothing worse for a man than the feeling of being useless. That was how my father felt. I was frozen. I think my body went into shock watching and hearing the torture of what was happening to my mother and sister. Just as I finally got enough courage to get up, I felt one of the men's foot on my neck holding me down so that I couldn't move. Then I felt the other man fondling me and pulling down my pants and before I knew it, I, too, was raped by both of these disgusting men.

Then both men walked over to my father and asked him if he enjoyed the show? Then they looked at each other and smiled in a very evil way. They started to untie my father, making him think that was what they were going to do before they took the money and jewelry and left. But that was not what happened. They told my father, "don't worry, we saved the best for last", threw him on the floor and once again each man raped my father.

They finally left, leaving us all in blood and tears. When my mother finally had enough strength, she got up to hold me and my sister. My father was still on the floor faced down and I could hear him crying. My mother heard him, too, and went to him. She held him for a while before the police and ambulance came. The paramedics told my mother that my father was in severe shock and they needed to get him to the hospital.

After some time had passed, my father was released from the hospital. However, he was never the same. Something died inside him that night. My parents sold everything they had and migrated to Canada. None of us felt safe in our home anymore and we all agreed that we needed to leave Trinidad. I left and never looked back.

Shortly after settling in Canada my father committed suicide. Even though my mother was devastated, she held me and my sister and told us that our father's mind was at peace now. She was able to tell us what was going on with our father now that he was no longer with us. She said that those horrible men took away his manhood. He hadn't felt like a man after that incident, only a failure. His job was to protect us and he was unable to that day. That filled him up with so much frustration and anger. Eventually it took him to the place where he took his own life.

My sister had been changed forever that day as well. So much so that she never let a man touch her again. She never moved on from that trauma and still remains single today. She lives close to me and we speak every night. She is now fifty-four while I am fifty-two years old. I was the opposite of my sister as I still believed in love and met the man of my dreams. Shortly after we had been dating, we decided to get married. I confided in my husband about what had happened to myself and family when we lived in Trinidad. After he just pulled me into his arms and told me that everything will be alright.

He was right because things did get better. We brought three beautiful babies into this world. They are the loves of our lives. They made me believe in purity again.

Thank you, Rah, for creating "Your Life Experiences with Rah" and giving us a safe place to share our stories.

"Many go through similar situations but not many can withstand reliving it everyday. I feel her family's pain. the mother who had to be the strongest from that moment onwards. the father who took this to his deathbed never felt a day of relief. Can we ever say we actually know what her father went through? Even if we put ourselves in his shoes, this is one that I would say I would not be able to figure out. I really close my eyes and pray that no one has to ever endure such pain in this world. one thing I realize from research is that some of the men that do these types of things had good families and that they were brought up in loving homes. What happens outside is where the triggers of hurting

innocent people come into play. hurting someone is not fun or nice - whether it be mentally or physically.

I am very happy she found a loving and peaceful life with less of life's challenges. It's hard and it's not easy going through these types of traumas but you can't give up. you can't stop living. your life and you are precious and you were put here for a purpose – sadly even if it's to go through that type of trauma to be able to help someone later on who is going through or went through a similar situation."

YLEWRAH

MY FATHER MADE ME HIS WIFE

I would just like to start off by saying what a wonderful job you are doing on the show " Your Life Experiences with Rah." I think it's amazing how all of these stories on your show are helping people going through similar experiences today. When I heard the story Fat Sweet Bottom, I questioned if I should send you my story? As you can guess, I decided to send it to you.

My mother passed away when I was only twelve years old. She had gone to the hospital one evening for severe stomach and chest pains. She had gotten to the hospital at 9 p.m. and by 8 a.m. the next morning she had gone to heaven. I hated my mother for dying while I was so young. I hated her for blessing me with her beautiful hazel eyes and for looking just like her. Most of all, I hated her for leaving me and enduring the horrible things my father would do to me after her passing, all because I looked just like her even though I was her son and not her daughter.

My father changed into a man I didn't know anymore after my mother died, till this day I am still not sure why my mother's passing sent my father into a strange behavior. My father worked at a factory which allowed him to take off for six months. He went into a depression and drank a lot during that time. My father and I were living in a village in Guyana where my father was financially stable. I remember leaving for school and coming home just to find my father where I had left him, drunk and asleep.

My mother's family tried to help out after my mother died, but my father wasn't nice to them and would just curse at them. I didn't get to see them that much as they lived far away. My father's family on the other hand did live close by, but no one on his side of the family got along. My grandfather on my father's side suffered from a stroke leaving him paralyzed on one side of his body. My grandmother on my father's side had passed away a few years after my grandfather's stroke.

I was blessed with a fat bottom just like the guy from the story, "Fat Sweet Bottom". At least I thought I was blessed until the worst happened and then I believed I was cursed and not at all blessed. It started to happen a year after my mother died. I had just turned thirteen. I was taking a bath when I heard my father yell out my name. I had told him I was in the bath and would be out soon. When I was done, I got out of the bath and wrapped myself in a towel. When I opened the bathroom door my father was standing there in just his underwear. I just assumed that he needed to use the bathroom and asked him why he didn't tell me that when he called out to me earlier? My father stared at me in a way he never had before. He was also mumbling something that I couldn't hear or understand. A strange feeling ran through my body as his look turned evil and he pulled off my towel. He pushed me onto the bathroom wall with my face to the wall. I had screamed for him to stop and asked him what had gotten into him, but he didn't answer me. Then I felt his erect penis press on my back side and I got really scared as I knew something was about to happen that should never happen between a parent and a child.

I felt my father's hot breath on my neck and his nose nestled on my ear when I felt his hand on my back and then onto my butt. He squeezed my butt cheeks together as he whispered that I got my butt from my mother and he was going to make good use of it. Hearing that gave me the strength somehow to escape the weight of his body on me and push him off of me. I ran into my room and locked the door. I cried and fell slowly down to the floor. I didn't know what to do or think. All I knew was how terrified I was. I was too afraid to sleep or move my body away from my bedroom door, fearing that if I did he would make his way in my room and I couldn't allow that to happen.

The following morning I didn't even eat breakfast. I just headed out the door to school with crazy thoughts about what had happened the night before. When I got home from school my father was gone. I thought he must be out drinking with his buddies and for now I am safe. So I went to take care of my daily chores. When I was done I headed towards my bedroom. After I entered my room all of the sudden I heard my bedroom door slam shut! I turned and saw my father standing there naked and erect.

My father told me not to scream and if I did that he would beat me so badly that I wouldn't be allowed to show my face in public. Now my father was masturbating in front of me. He looked at me and slammed me onto my bed face down. The first thing I felt was his hard penis on my back. That's when I cried out for him to stop, I begged him to. He didn't stop and I heard him calling out my mother's name and not mine. That's when I realized my father wasn't seeing his son when he looked at me, rather he was seeing his wife!

I couldn't believe my father was doing what he was doing to me. I had always looked at him like my protector and now he was abusing me in a way I never thought he would. I tried not to allow the worst to happen. I had squeezed my butt cheeks as hard as I could so that he wouldn't be able to enter me. When my father felt how tight I was, he grabbed the coconut oil by my bed and rubbed it into his hands before he inserted two of his fingers inside of me. It felt like a razor blade was cutting into my insides. I thought how that had been the worst pain I ever felt and then there was a bigger pain! He inserted his penis into me and he wasn't gentle. He slammed it into me over and over again which felt like he was ripping me into two. I screamed louder than I had ever screamed before. I screamed out so loud that I thought I would pass out, but I didn't. I wished I would have died that night.

This continued for a year. It got less aggressive as he wasn't drinking as much, but it was still going on. My father had really lost it. He was no longer calling me by my name, as he was calling me by my mother's name. It was as if I was the one who had died a few years ago and not my mother. I even started to call him by his name and no longer Dad. Maybe I was losing it at this point as well? You see he had kept me locked in the house and I wasn't allowed out, not even to go to school. I was trying everything for him to allow me to get out of that house and back to school.

He finally agreed and I was allowed to go back to school. One afternoon as I was walking home from school, I stopped under a tree for some shade as the sun was hot and the walk to my house was a bit far. I heard the old lady speaking to her granddaughter, telling her that she must always pray to Lord Shiva and to talk to him like a friend. I questioned who this man named Shiva was? Somehow hearing the old lady telling her granddaughter to start off the prayer saying, "Om Namah Shivaya" *(this is a powerful mantra in hinduism and hindus believe as shiva is the male form of devi durga and the lord)* repeatedly stayed with me and as I continued my way home I repeated that prayer over and over. When I got into the house, I broke down crying as all I saw were the disgusting things my father had done to me in the past few months. I started to beg this Shiva to help solve my problems and protect me from this beast of a man known as my father. I begged Shiva to take me away from that place.

That evening my father had arrived home sober even though it was very late. He went straight to bed without even looking at me or saying anything to me. So the next day I continued to pray to Lord Shiva and everyday after that. A week of praying had passed and my father didn't hurt me during that time.

Fast forward to June when school was ending and summer would begin with nowhere for me to go during the day. On my last day of school when I got home, my father had turned into a beast again as he was drunk! He told me to go into the bathroom and that he needed to talk with me. I went to the bathroom and prayed to Lord Shiva not to let my father hurt me again. I turned and there was my father naked holding the belt. He threatened me with the belt in the past that if I didn't do what he wanted he would strike me with it.

I had closed my eyes and thought over and over again, Om Namah Shivaya when I heard a knock at the door. At first my father ignored it, but then the knock got louder. So he quickly got dressed and answered the door. It was my aunt, my mother's sister from Canada. I hadn't seen her since I was eleven. I ran out of the bathroom and into her arms. She told me that she had made a promise to my mother that as soon as she was settled in Canada that she would come and get me. My father at first wasn't allowing me to go. He kept telling her that without my help around the house he wouldn't survive. My aunt told him she wasn't stealing him from him and that I was his son, not his wife. She told him that she could guarantee that his son would have a great future with her. She went on to say to my father how when I was born it was the best day of his life and that he only wanted the best for me.

My father turned to look at me as he fell to the ground in shame for the things he had done to me that he could never erase from either of our brains. He then told my aunt to take me. My aunt looked at my father with a weird face. She wasn't sure what was going on? My father said he couldn't lose me after he lost his wife. My aunt just turned to him and told him he was being silly. That she wasn't taking me from him, she was only taking me to live with her so that I could have a better life. She told him that I would come back to visit and one day my father could come to Canada and live with us there.

I got what I needed and got into my aunt's car without looking back. I didn't even stop to say goodbye to my father. When my aunt got in the car, I asked her to tell me about Lord Shiva. She smiled at me and told me that my mother would say she knew that one day Lord Shiva would show her and her family miracles. She started to believe after her friend was saved by a tall stranger. This stranger had saved her friend from being run over by a car as she was crossing the street. Had it not been for the stranger that pushed her friend aside from that moving car, she would've been dead. She then drove us to a little Hindu church. She had known the people at the church and expressed to them how intrigued I was with Lord Shiva. An old man came over to me and gave me a small picture of Lord Shiva. Till this day, I still have that picture which is framed now in my home. The old man had told me to never lose faith, even when things seemed hopeless. He told me to always pray to Lord Shiva with all of my heart and that if I did, my troubles would be taken away and my wishes would come true.

I'm older now as you could assume. I married my wife when I was eighteen. I told her everything that had happened between my father and I after my mother passed. She never looked at me differently after hearing my story. Our children knew that I had been physically abused by their grandfather but I never went into all of the details with them. They didn't need to know that. I just wanted them to know their father as a whole and I also wanted them to know that what I went through was wrong. That way if something that bad ever happened to them they would know that they could come talk to their mother or myself.

As far as what happened to my father after I left, I heard he remarried and had a daughter. I wish he had believed in the Lord Shiva, if not for him, for my step-mother. He abused her. Karma came for him, though. One afternoon while he was on their roof fixing something, he apparently slipped and fell. That is what his wife told everyone. Some people believe she had had enough and she pushed him off of the roof. No one really knows, nor did they care to investigate. From that fall, he became paralyzed and could no longer speak yet he was aware of everything going on around him.

Lord Shiva had not been done punishing him for all his wrongs after that fall. During that same year, robbers invaded his house, tied him up and made him watch as they raped his wife and daughter in front of him. A few years after that he died.

Rah, I heard you say on your show that you are a spiritual person and that you believe in karma. I continue to pray to Lord Shiva and now I will pray to him that your show will reach millions of followers. It will help people and you will become a very successful man.

"Every time I read this story, I cry. I cry as I feel his pain and see what he has endured. your children are part of you, and they didn't ask you to come into this world. I say these things over and over : the world is overpopulated, and it should take two consenting adults who planned and strategized to bring a child into this world with a long-term plan. If not, adopt and give a child a home and love them like you love yourself. sadly, things weren't like that in those times, and the things that happened to him happened. angels do exist. They exist in the form of humans. As mentioned in the past, a famous quote that people take for granted, "when god can't come, he sends…" is so true. you are only given how much you can handle or take or juggle. We know some can't handle it, and sometimes, sadly, they take their own lives. The truth is the problems of life do come to an end, meaning the issues you had from yesterday will be gone while other new ones come to challenge you. be strong and know it will be alright soon. believe this and believe in yourself because only you can help yourself out of whatever is going on with you."

YLEWRAH

MOTHER'S ARE GOD'S ANGELS ON THIS EARTH

Rah, I love listening to your show and all of the different stories I hear on Your Life Experiences with Rah. A lot include stories of mothers who disown their children. My story is about my mother and what a mother she was. If she wasn't a good parent, my sister would've been emotionally hurt or killed. My life was a blessing as well and I owe all that to my mother.

This is my story. My mother was a very brave woman and she always put my sister and myself first, no matter what. My father was the opposite of my mother. He would physically and emotionally beat my mother. My mother stayed with him because he was the father of her children and she didn't want to take our father away from us. That was until he started to abuse us. My mother couldn't see her children in pain, not the pain she had endured for years. She picked up her two small children and left, knowing what a financial struggle that would be for her. That's why I always considered my mother to be the strongest person I knew.

My mother's brother took us in. My mother only knew her brother to be a kind-hearted person like herself. However, no one knows someone's true colors until they live with them. My aunt apparently had been going through the same thing my mother had gone through with her family. I guess women grow up thinking they have to obey their husbands no matter what. I hope my future daughters will never have to go through what my mother or aunt had to.

When my mother confronted my uncle about what he was doing to his wife, he just justified his abuse by saying my aunt wasn't a good person.

My mother and I knew that was a lie. We were all living under one roof and saw that what my uncle said just wasn't true.

My mother would work at a poultry depot on the weekends. I would work there on Sundays to help her save up money to eventually get our own place. My younger sister who was twelve at the time would help our aunt around the house with chores while we were working. One Sunday my aunt left my sister home to do the chores because she had to go take care of her mother who had fallen ill. My sister would always greet us at the door and for whatever reason that Sunday she didn't. All of a sudden we heard a loud scream coming from the backyard. We ran to see what was going on and when we got there we saw that my uncle was naked and ripping off my sister's dress. My sister was hysterical, screaming for him to let her go and not to hurt her. She was begging him to get off of her!

My mother out of instinct picked up a pipe that was on the ground and without thinking, she flew towards her brother screaming to get off of her daughter! What I saw was a mama bear protecting her young daughter no matter what the cost was. She was beating her brother with that pipe. My uncle didn't even see it coming. Somehow he escaped and ran through the neighborhood but naked screaming for help! He tried to convince everyone that my mother had gone mad and to help him! They didn't know what to do or who to believe. Eventually the truth came out about what my uncle would've done to my baby sister had my mother not been brave enough to stand up to him and protect her daughter.

My mother once again packed herself and her two children up to move away from another beast. This time she took her sister-in-law with her. She knew her brother would come back and will be angry. She wasn't leaving without my aunt. We all moved in with my grandmother. Thankfully my aunt came with us. We found out later that my uncle was a coke addict from one of her neighbors and that she had gotten out in the nick of time.

A few days after moving into my grandmother's house, we learned that my uncle hung himself. I guess the shame of what he had done all those years to my aunt and what he was about to do to my sister was too much for him and he took his own life.

Both my sister and mother are no longer on this Earth. My mother passed away ten years ago from a heart attack. My sister was a lucky girl and had a great life thanks to my mother. She had an angelic man as a husband. The opposite of what my father and uncle were. Sadly my sister died three years ago from cancer.

What I learned from my mother is how to be a loving parent. That your children once they are born come first in this world. My wish by sharing my story is that more parents will be like my mother. Without her I don't think I would've become a good man. Had she stayed with my father I could've just as easily become like him, a man who beats his own wife and children. A man I would've been ashamed of becoming.

Thank you, Rah, and to all of your #RAHSTAZ (FANS) for letting me share my story.

"I am grateful as well as thankful you shared this story so others can read and know when enough is enough or when to stand up to the "beast" in our lives. no matter what the form that "beast" takes, even if it's not human, remember you have the strength within yourself to make everything right and to get out of the situation you are in."

YLEWRAH

LOVE RAPE RELATIONSHIP

I would like to thank you for the show "Your Life Experiences with Rah." Your show has helped me to understand that what I did was not wrong and to not have any regrets. I hope my story will help others going through the same pain that I had to endure and to know that you are not alone.

I am just a regular normal Caribbean woman who isn't that educated. I always respected my parents and grew up believing whatever your parents said is the best for you. When I was eighteen going on nineteen years of age my parents arranged my marriage to an older man who was almost forty!

My family was not a rich family, but we were comfortable. My husband and his family on the other side were. They sold jewelry and gold and therefore had money. Even though they had money, no one was happy. It's true what they say, money cannot buy you love. My husband's family was proof of that statement.

I grew up in a very loving family. My father never hit my mother or his kids. So when my husband hit me for the first time I was lost with emotion. I never experienced that and didn't know how to go about that, after all he was my husband. As time went on a slap here and there became a beating here and there. The first time he bit me while he was beating me. I still have the scar from that bite. The beating was so bad it caused my first miscarriage. The reason for that beating didn't make sense to me and I'm sure it won't make sense to whoever is reading this either. I had asked my husband's brother's wife who was working at a company if she could get me a position there as a bookkeeper since I had some accounting background from school. My husband believed the only reason why I wanted a job was to find another man. I was in shock that he thought that was why I wanted to work. I paid for questioning his thought process being beaten up and that cost me my unborn child.

I ran away after that incident to my parents home. I knew what my husband did was wrong and I thought my parents would understand why I left. My parents were very traditional and believed that once you were married that was it. No matter what the problems are, you work through them. For two weeks my husband begged both me and my parents for me to come home. He told us that he made a mistake and that he would never hurt me again. My father told me I was married and that I had to work through the rough patch and not walk away, so I went back to my husband. I told my husband I would only come back if he allowed me to work, which he agreed to.

After six months of working I found out I was pregnant again. The problem was my husband thought I cheated on him with someone at work because he didn't believe the baby was his. Therefore, he choked me this time while he beat me. He did this by tying the bedsheet around my neck and hung me from the post of the bed. While I was dangling, he hit my stomach over and over. Each time he punched or kicked my belly, he would say that I cheated on him and the baby I was carrying wasn't his. Yes, this caused me to lose my second child in a hurtful and sad way.

Two and half years later I was still married and pregnant for the third time. Thankfully during this pregnancy my husband's rage and jealousy had calmed down and we brought a beautiful baby girl into the world. For a short time we were happy and I thought things would be ok.

A year later my husband wanted me to join him in attending his friend's party. I didn't want to go because I knew my husband would drink and get drunk at the party which meant there would be a good chance of my husband beating me that evening. He beat me anyway for telling him that I didn't want to go to the party. This time I got a bloody red eye.

A few days before that beating I had bumped into a man at work accidentally. He had seen marks on my neck and hand from previous beatings. He asked me what happened but I didn't tell him. After the recent beating there was no denying where I got my bloody red eye from. I just started to cry and ended up telling him all that I have been through since I got married. He told me that he was going to get his visa the following week to go to the USA and begged me to go with him. I explained I couldn't leave my daughter behind. He told me he didn't expect me to leave her behind. I found out what I needed for both myself and my daughter to get our visa without any suspicion. In those times all you needed was a big bank statement and a good letter from your job to get your child's visa. All was done and the three of us left Trinidad and went to live our lives in the USA.

I thought this man was my savior, my angel. We were happy for six years and even had a son together. My daughter even adjusted to her new life. She never asked about or where her Daddy was. She was aware of what her father did to her mother. Unfortunately she witnessed some of the beatings I took.

My angel liked to drink Johnny Walker on the rocks. Sometimes he could finish a whole bottle in less than an hour! One day while he was off from work, I had gone into work that morning but wasn't feeling well so I came home early. The kids were still in school. I came home to see my angel watching pornography while masturbating. He turned it off when he saw that I was home early. He walked over to me and pushed me against the wall. He started to rip off my clothes very aggressively. I tried to push him off of me as he had never been this rough when it came to sex before. This didn't feel like love and I didn't want this, not this way. I kept on asking him what was wrong with him and to please stop, but he didn't. Instead he grabbed my body and slammed me onto the floor while tearing my panties off. This was the first time he raped me. When it was over, he just lay there before he passed out. When I felt it was safe, I got up and took a shower. I need to scrub off that horrible memory. I couldn't believe this just happened. I thought this man was my angel who saved me from my ex-husband who would torture me over and over. Now this man just raped me with no remorse.

Days had passed and neither of us had spoken about the horrible incident. I think part of him was ashamed that he had committed such a crime regardless of the fact that he was drunk. He knew that wasn't an excuse for what he did to me. One night he tried to kiss me, but I still couldn't allow him to touch me. Everything was different now. A few nights later he eased his way to touch me while kissing my neck. He then started to undress me. He told me that he wanted to play a game with me. He was being sweet and kissing me in a loving way that I gave in and agreed to play the game that he wanted. He told me to repeat after him, "I want you to rape my asshole and I want you to fuck me till I shit myself. I want you to rape my ass and make it bleed."

I heard this and pushed him off of me asking him to stop. I told him I wasn't going to say that. He started to kiss my lips and told me that he loves me and that he needed me to just say it. That it is only a game, to please play just this once. So I started to say it and he told me I wasn't saying it right. He turned me over so that I was face down in the bed and he told me to say it again and louder and like I meant it. As I said it, I started to get really mad that I screamed it really loud. I heard him say to me that he doesn't really want to do those things to me, it's just a turn on hearing me say that. He asked if I believed him because that was some sick shit if I thought he really wanted to do those things to me. Then he asked me to repeat it one more time but louder. Of course, I did what he asked of me.

He then pushed my face into the pillow and I felt him spit into my ass. He started to penetrate me roughly. I told him to stop, but he held my head down so hard that I couldn't even breathe. He then did what I screamed for him to do and raped my ass. He pushed himself so hard into me that I even shit on myself. That still didn't make him stop. When he was done he passed out, just like the last time. I lay there for a while. I was in a lot of pain and couldn't move just yet. When I was able to move, I crawled my way into the bathroom to take a shower. I just sat there with the water hitting my head and body as I held myself and cried. I even passed out for a while in the shower from all the trauma that just happened.

The next morning I got up and got dressed to get my kids ready for school. He was still passed out and I had no desire to wake him. After I dropped off the kids at school, I went down to the precinct to report that this man had now raped me twice. Of course the cops questioned it, since I never reported the first rape and I was still living with him. I explained how we had been living together for over 6 years and shared a four year old son as well as my daughter from a previous relationship. The cops did put in a call to him over the allocations I was accusing him of.

When I got home he was mad. He told the kids to go to their room because mommy and daddy needed some alone time. He walked me into our bedroom. Once we were in there, he slammed our bedroom door and locked it. He then pushed me up against the door and asked if I thought

I could fuck with him? He played a recording of me begging him to rape me until I shit myself. That recording also had him saying to me that he would never do the things I was asking him to do to me. That son of a bitch knew I would go to the cops and that he needed back-up. He then put his hands around my neck and choked me. As he was choking me he told me that if I ever tried that shit again that he would rape my daughter or even our son and that he would do it right in front of me.

I pleaded for him not to hurt the children. I told him he could rape me or do anything he wants but to not harm the kids. So that's just what he did. He ordered me to take my clothes off and stand facing the wall. He then beat me with his belt while crying, asking me why I was making him do this to me? He then raped me. This man was no longer my angel. He was an unstoppable dangerous monster that I didn't know.

Things got worse. Not only was he now beating me before he raped me, I was now his human ashtray as he would put out his cigars on my body. For six months I took this emotional and physical abuse. I knew the only way to stop him from hurting me was to take some action, but that meant that I would have to take the law into my own hands and I would have to trick him. So one day while the kids were at school and he was home from work, I made sure I was home with him. I told him that we needed to talk. I told him I was changing and that he was making me a different person. I walked over to him and pulled down his pants. As I did that, I told him I wanted him to rape me. I told him that I needed him to. I left work early because it was all I could think of. I begged him to rape my ass until I shit on myself. He slapped me to the ground shouting at me that he was in charge. He grabbed me by my hair and dragged me to the bedroom. He was hurting me. I begged him not to rape me again, that he was my husband and I loved him. He told me to shut up and that he was going to make me shit myself.

What he didn't know was that I had gotten myself a small but extremely sharp buck knife that was by the side of the bed where he always raped me. I jumped on top of my husband in such a surprise and stabbed him four times in his chest! When he fell to the floor bleeding, I cut off half of his dick. He lost conscience from all the blood loss. My intentions were never to kill him. I couldn't go to jail and leave my two children behind. I called 911 and asked for an ambulance. The cops came and said that I needed to come down to the station for questioning. I had recorded everything this time. In that recording, you hear me begging him not to rape right after hearing him tell me he was going to rape me.

However, I had to pay for my crimes as well. Three months later a cop knocked on my door and I was arrested. I was on trial for two and a half years! During that time my children were placed in foster care. Thankfully the judge for my hearing was a woman. She said my crime has already been completed. That being away from my kids for that long was punishment enough. As for him, he was denied any kind or visitation rights. I was just happy that he was never able to touch my children or hurt me ever again. The recording I took of him saying what he was going to do to me helped my case and he was locked up.

Rah, the last two of your shows that I watched helped me to decide to share my story with you. They also helped me to see that what I did was to protect myself and my children and that I didn't have a choice.

I moved to Georgia now and my son is a grown man. I pray every day that he never follows in his father's footsteps of abusing women. I don't think he will, though. He's in the navy and they will teach him the kind of healthy discipline he needs and will come out of it as a good man. Also, I have seen him with my daughter's children. He has always been so kind and gentle with them which always puts a smile on my face and in my heart. As for myself, I never remarried. Nor have I dated that much. After those two horrible experiences, I don't think I will ever be able to trust another man in this lifetime.

I hope that any women out there going through what I did know that they aren't alone. I'm sure I'm not the first or the last woman to go through what I did. Just because he is your husband, that doesn't mean he has the right to hit you or rape you. If he does it once, he will do it again. There's so much help out there, use it!

"I love her and her advice is golden. It is very true that there is help out there if you are going through anything like she did. when you think one major trouble is over and it can't get worse it just gets crazier at times and saying you get only what you can handle is an understatement here. she should never have had to go through all that she did. This was betrayal and

hurt to the utmost. I am so happy she was smart enough to learn and do the same to save her life and her children. In this world, in every religion, they speak of the devil and demons, but the reality of it is there's no devil or demons as decided as in these stories - the true evil is man himself. a man with a mind to tell him right from wrong and lead him into the right direction but they chose to do these sad hurtful things thereby hurting innocent lives and destroying them mentally and physically."

YLEWRAH

LAST BBQ

Rah, I know you must hear this all of the time but I'm going to tell you as well: You are doing an excellent job with Your Life Experiences with Rah. One of my friends introduced me to Anonymous Monday's. I caught the episode about you speaking about race and I loved what you said. Again, you are doing a great job! Keep it up! I wish that I could be a guest on your show one of these days.

My family and I are originally from Detroit and of Haitian background. My husband was a high school drop out. Later on, in life he got his high school diploma. We started dating when we were both nineteen. We actually shared the same birthday. My husband met up with an old friend from high school regarding employment right before the financial crisis of 2008. He started out as an insurance agent when he met up with another old friend at a business conference. That's when he was offered a position on Wall Street, but that meant we would have to move to New York. So we moved from Detroit to New York. After six months he was a financial service professional overseeing some really big accounts. My husband would help to protect the assets of others. He would help his clients with retirement planning, life insurance, college funding, etc.

My husband was now not only married to me, but also to his work. He spent most of his time working. He worked more than spending time at home. We were living in a two bedroom apartment in Brooklyn. My husband was working really hard at that time. Things got bad at times due to the economy. There were a lot of deals that he couldn't close. However, he never gave up because he knew there was money to be made and he went after it.

His hard work did pay off, because in 2012 we were able to purchase a beautiful house in Long Island. It was a different kind of life living on the Island and it took a bit for myself and the children to get used to it. I had been working as a receptionist when we lived in Brooklyn. My husband kept on pressuring me to quit, especially once we moved out to Long Island. Thank God I didn't listen to him and still had a job.

You see this is where I could relate to some of those other stories that I watched on Your Anonymous Monday's show. No, I didn't catch my husband with some other woman bent over on a desk. I was left with something much worse. It's been three years now since my husband had gone up to heaven. My kids and I miss him dearly. July 4, 2014 was our last family BBQ together. My husband was grilling when he just fell to the ground suddenly. He had major lung failure. He had been a heavy smoker. I tried to get him to quit, but he wouldn't listen to me. He was in and out of the hospital for months after being diagnosed with lung cancer.

The day of my husband's funeral after his cremation everyone had headed back to the house. This is when I got the first surprise. One of his co-workers whom I had met once at a work event started to question me about another woman who was at the funeral with a toddler. I did notice the child, but I was a bit out of it as I had just lost my husband of many years and was putting him down to rest. My only concern at the time was for my own children. Turns out that the woman with the toddler was my husband's mistress and the toddler was theirs. I lost it right there in front of everyone when the speculations were confirmed by this woman. I feel bad looking back now about how mean I was and all the horrible things I said to her. As it turned out we became very close friends and I love her child as one of my own.

Rah, my husband had a job to oversee and to protect people's assets and to make sure that the other individuals lives and futures were secure. However, the son of a bitch did not secure his children's or wife's future financially.

Rah, I no longer could have afforded to keep up with our lifestyle now that my husband was gone. The mortgage for our house was not possible for me to keep up with on my salary alone. I had to sell it and I didn't make that much of a profit either. It did, however, help me to pay more than half for a three bedroom co-op in Brooklyn. He never took out life insurance on himself, nor did he set up any funding for college for the kids.

Even though my husband had made a decent living, all of his money went to the medical bills for his care before he died. Thankfully I never quit my job and I had savings. I miss my husband everyday and my children and I are still adjusting to life without him. My life has changed since he passed. Now each morning when I wake, I thank God for another living day.

A few months after my husband passed away I was extremely busy with work and now playing the role of Mom and Dad. I thought I was just over stressed. My friend, my husband's mistress, convinced me to go to the doctor to make sure it was just stress. Turns out I wasn't so run down from stress - I was HIV positive. This was the last thing my husband gave me. His mistress was also HIV positive. Did my husband know that he was HIV positive before he died? It would make sense since he deteriorated so quickly once he was diagnosed with lung cancer.

I am so grateful for my husband's mistress, as weird as that sounds. We are in this together, battling this disease together. We are holding on for a cure and living each day as if it is the last.

My wish for others reading my story is to please have safe sex and do not cheat. Just takes one time for not only yourself to get HIV, but to give it to your partner who was being faithful and didn't deserve to get a life-threatening disease.

"Men or women should not have to endure this type of betrayal to begin with. If you are a man or woman and in a relationship, the day you feel it's not working or you need to go out and find more than you feel you have in your current relationship ends the one you have. oh, yes, it might be easier said than done and easier to cheat or keep the "hidden secrets" to yourselves but somehow the darkness is removed by light "whatever is in the dark comes to light". the truth does come out and when it does, please think about the people that you hurt. this woman had gotten hurt by losing her husband whom she found out was cheating and had an outside child — and to even further find out he left her with a death penalty if left untreated which she never asked for.

I NAMED MY DAUGHTER AFTER MY BEST FRIEND

Hey, Rah,

My story is about my best friend. We met in high school. I knew she was going to be somebody who would be very special in my life. Our friendship blossomed very quickly as she was easy to talk to and I was able to trust her. I had a boyfriend that was already in my life before I met her. Gradually, the three of us became inseparable. We would go to the mall, to the river and to the beach just to name a few things we did together.

When I was eighteen my father sat me down and told me that he needed to discuss something very important with me. He told me I was getting married! I was in shock. Why? Who was this person I was marrying? He explained it was going to be an arranged marriage. I explained that I couldn't do that because I was already in love. My father was not sympathetic. He got very angry with me and told me that I didn't have a choice and that I would go through with the marriage because the agreement with my future wife's family had already been agreed upon.

I felt heartbroken. I ran over to my boyfriend's house to tell him what was going on. I begged him to come and speak to my father. I wanted him to ask my father for permission to marry me. He was terrified of my father and didn't think that was a good idea. Rather, he thought the best decision was for us to break up. He told me that it would kill him to see me marrying another man, but that we didn't have a choice as the arrangement had already been decided upon. He saw me tearing up and that I was in so much pain about us not being able to be together, that he finally agreed to speak with my father. As we approached my house my father was at the gate and he looked very angry. As we got closer to my father, he started to yell at me and said that I was a very stubborn girl. My boyfriend calmly asked him if they could speak. My father agreed. My boyfriend told my father that he was very in love with his daughter and asked if he could marry me. My father's response to him was how could he be a good husband to his daughter at only nineteen if he didn't even have a job? My father's concern was that he would still have to support his daughter and now her husband if he agreed. In our culture, once you are married, your parents are no longer financially responsible for you. My father didn't see this happening if he agreed to my boyfriend marrying me. My boyfriend understood my father's concerns and told him that he already had a plan. He was planning on moving to Minnesota in America and there was work for him there. He guaranteed that his daughter would be well taken care of not only financially but emotionally as well. Yet my father still had concerns. He knew the only way to handle this was through a game of cricket. He told my boyfriend whoever wins in the game will get their wish granted. Even though my boyfriend hated sports and never played cricket, he agreed.

They met at noon the next day to play cricket. I stayed home as I wasn't allowed to go. I waited patiently for my father to come home. When he did, I looked up and saw the smile on his face and knew I had to go through with the arranged marriage. My eyes filled up with water and I ran out of the house and straight over to my best friend's house. I needed advice from someone I could trust. I knew she would understand as she was going through a similar situation. She was seeing someone who she was very much in love with. The problem was that he was Muslim and she was Hindu. Because her boyfriend wasn't Hindu, she knew her father would never agree to them marrying. She just embraced me in a long hug that we both needed. We both knew we could never marry the people we were actually in love with.

The man I was arranged to marry was twelve years older than me. My whole life changed rapidly after we were married. He lived in Guyana and since I was now his wife, I had to move there with him and his family. I didn't know that I was pregnant when I got married. When I put the time line together I knew the baby was my boyfriend's baby, but I also knew that was a secret I would have to take to my grave. It would've destroyed my family as well as my husband's family had they known the truth. I also feared they would have taken the baby from me and wasn't sure what would've happened to me. So I waited a few weeks before I told my husband that I was pregnant. I had to make him believe that it was our child. No one questioned the baby being born a month early as it was everyone's impression that I had been a virgin when I married my husband. So everyone thought my son just came early. I loved my son so much from the moment he was put into my arms.

Our marriage was going well for the first three years. We were enjoying raising my son together. However, he started to travel to America for work. I noticed when he had come back to Guyana from America that he had an unusual mark on his neck. When I questioned him about it he slapped me hard on my face. He told me how dare I accuse him of such things. Two days later he came home late from work and he was very drunk. I asked him where he had been - that he couldn't have been at work that late. I should've known not to ask. My husband beat me severely that night. Him being drunk made him more aggressive. The beating was so bad that I couldn't leave my house for days. I started to hate my husband. After all, I never loved him.

A few months later I found out I was pregnant. I went to the doctor and begged him to give me something to miscarry. This man had beaten me repeatedly almost every night. I didn't want to bring a child, let alone his into this world. Unfortunately, the doctor told me that was impossible as I was already five months along. So I had to go home and tell him that I was pregnant. I thought he would've been happy but I was wrong. He immediately started to beat me. He believed the child wasn't his and he was trying to kill it inside of me. After my husband passed out that night, I grabbed my son and left without ever looking back.

I knew after my husband started to beat me that eventually this day would come so I had slowly started to save enough money for me to be able to take my son and leave. I traveled back home to my best friend's house. I was afraid to go to my family's house, as I feared my husband would come looking for us and that would've been the first place he looked. My best friend took us in and took care of us for a few days. Her uncle helped me to arrange for myself and my child to travel to America. Even though I was very relieved that I was able to escape from my husband, my life without him financially supporting us was very hard. I was now a single mom raising two children in a foreign country. After three years of struggling, life became easier.

I had become very friendly with a woman from work. Her brother was getting married one weekend and she invited me to the celebration. It was a small get together in their backyard. I arrived a little bit late with my son. My daughter was home with a babysitter. As I approached the backyard I heard a familiar voice telling the other guys about his story and why till this day he has remained single - that he could never love again the way he loved the girl that was taken from him. I couldn't believe it. Not only was the love of my life steps away from me, but after all these years without any communication he had been waiting for me. I swelled up with tears and I started to uncontrollably cry. I was sobbing so loud at that point that everyone turned to look at me and my son. My love ran over to me and pulled me into a hug and twirled me around. After he put me down, I bent down to tell my son to look up and meet his real daddy. Now it was my love's turn for his eyes to fill up with tears. He heard what I told my son and realized that he was his. He bent down to introduce himself to his child and embraced him in a hug.

I am now in my fifties and have had a lot of love in my life after that day. My three children. Yes, you read that correctly. We had another child together. All three are fully grown now and I even have grandchildren.

I wish I could tell you that my best friend had a happy ending with the man she was in love with. Unfortunately, I can't. Her father never gave them his blessing to wed. They both decided if they couldn't be together that they could die together. They didn't want to live unless they could be married. They say every time someone passes, a child is born. The day my daughter was born was the day my best friend took her life. She and her boyfriend drank poison and fell asleep holding hands. I ended up naming my daughter after my best friend.

> *"The rules that applied in the past were so ridiculous that some worked out fine and some just didn't. I always say true love exists and it happens with the right person and the right*

moment. all you have to do is it comes with a lot of baggage and you have to be ready to handle it and continue that love story. No man is perfect and so is any relationship, as people aren't the same. you must understand each other if you really want to make it ahead. Sometimes in life when we don't get certain things we want it is a blessing as well as a curse. don't stress over what didn't happen and what could have happened - always think about the positives like your best friend. you held her so close to your heart she was returned to you, whether you realize it or not .

Always look for the small light as it tries to come in when all we see is darkness in life."

YLEWRAH

FAMILY SECRETS

Rah, what I love most about watching Your Life Experiences with Rah is how real it is. Some of the stories I have heard have made me laugh, some have made me angry and some have touched my heart so much that I tear up hearing your #rahstaz(FANS) stories. So many people have opened up on your show and have not been judged and therefore I feel comfortable enough to share mine with you.

My story is about my brother. I loved him and he was my hero. Unfortunately not all of my family saw him in the same light, especially our father.

We grew up in a small village in Guyana. There was a very poor culture. We planted vegetables and caught fish for a living. My brother at a young age left home and found work. Not too long after he left home he found the love of his life. My brother would come to visit occasionally yet he never brought his significant other to meet us which I had found strange. A year later when I was fifteen my brother stayed home with us for about a month. This visit was different. My brother wasn't happy during this time. He was drinking a lot and he was very sad. One night I found my brother drunk and crying, so I asked him to please open up to me and tell me what was wrong? He broke down and told me that the person he's been in love with wasn't with another woman; it was with a man. After he confided in me he begged me not to tell our parents. I promised him that I would keep his secret.

A year later my brother came back home for a visit. This time he had a beautiful woman by his side. He came to ask for our parents' blessing as he planned on marrying her. I was a little confused. A year ago he told me he was in love with a man and now he's marrying a woman? I hugged him and was about to ask him what happened, but he just smiled and told me that she loves him and that it is all that matters. He went on to say it was what was best for their family.

His fiancé was from Guyana as well. She and her family had migrated to Florida at a young age. She seemed like a nice woman with respect and she cared about my brother, which in my eyes was all that mattered.

They welcomed a son into the world a year after their marriage. Three years later my brother visited us again and to tell my entire family how they can move to America to live with his family and their two year old son. Two years later my family and I migrated to Queens, New York. With the help of my brother's in-laws, my parents were able to find employment and I was able to continue with my education.

We had been living with my brother and his family for a few weeks when we noticed the distance between him and his wife. My brother now had two children and yet he was sleeping in the basement rather than with his wife.

My family and I were under the impression that my brother's wife had cheated on him in the past. I pondered if that was what was going on again? About a month later my parents asked their son and daughter-in-law what was going on. Why was there so much tension between them? My sister-in-law turned to her husband and told him that he should be the one to tell his family what was going on. I don't know what happened, but I just blurted out that the tension was because my sister-in-law cheated on my brother again. I will never forget how pale she got and how tears swelled up her eyes with my accusation. She turned to me and said, "I'm sorry that is what you think, the truth is, in fact, I never cheated on your brother. He has been the one who has cheated on this family for years now." My brother didn't deny this. He couldn't look at us so he just put his head down on the table. My sister-in-law went on to tell us the real story of what had been going on. She told us that her cousin had been staying with them for a few months. During that time your brother became very close with my cousin which I originally was happy about. I would've never expected that their friendship would be anything more than that, but I was wrong. One day I came home and found my cousin having sex with your brother. I was in shock and didn't know what to do. Finally I kicked my own cousin out of my house.

Our father was distraught. I saw the anger all over his face. He couldn't believe what he was hearing. The story got worse as it turned out my brother met and fell in love with his wife's cousin years before they had even met. They had become lovers while still living in Guyana. My brother was introduced to his wife through her cousin when he decided to marry a woman and move to Florida. My sister-in-law was now in tears. She finally told her story. She no longer had to keep her husband's secret. She went on to tell us as much as she wants to hate her husband, she can't because of their two children.

Now my brother was sobbing hearing his wife telling his family the entire truth. He was screaming saying how ashamed he was for falling in love with the same sex, for disappointing his family and for hurting his wife the way he did. My father heard my brother say all this and instead of comforting his son in his arms, he just ran over to him in such a rage and punched my brother in the face. He just kept on punching him and wouldn't stop even though my mother and I tried to stop him. When we finally were able to get my father off of him, my brother just got up and left.

It was a month before anyone heard from my brother after that night. He got in contact with me and asked if I would meet him. We met at a local coffee shop. He told me how much he missed his wife and kids and hoped they were ok. He started to get very emotional and I could see that he was embarrassed with all the people watching him. So I told him we could go back to his place so that he could talk more freely. He was renting a basement apartment in Brooklyn. In the cab he broke down in tears and couldn't stop crying. My heart ached for him. Rah, even now as I tell you about my story, I can still feel my brother's pain that day in the cab.

When we finally arrived at my brother's apartment, he told me more heart-breaking news about what had happened to him. When he had to still live in Guyana, one of our uncles would take him into the fields and rape him day after day. That was one of the reasons why he stayed away. He continued to tell me that his lover, his wife's cousin, was never a faithful person. His lover's wife had been ill for a few months and was diagnosed with HIV. My brother had gotten his blood test results back and sadly he had contracted the virus, too. He was very grateful that his wife had tested negative.

My brother begged me once again to keep his secret and not tell our parents. Three years later my brother started to get very sick. Both of his kidneys were damaged and he needed a kidney transplant. My mother and I both got tested but neither was a match. Somehow, even though my father still wanted nothing to do with my brother we convinced him to get

     RAHUL K. MAHARAJ

tested. My father was a match! My brother had hope. That was until his doctor spoke with our father and reviewed everything with him. He told my father about my brother having HIV. After hearing this my father told the doctor that the deal was off. He was not giving up one of his kidneys to someone who was going to die anyway. He was furious.

The rest of my brother's life, if you can even call it that was very hard to watch. His body started to shut down and he suffered in a lot of pain towards the end. I never saw my brother as someone different. I saw him as someone who lived a harder life. I never stopped loving my brother, not even hearing his secrets. I made sure my nephews knew what a good man their father was and thanked my sister-in-law for staying by my brother's side towards the end. I will always be grateful to her for the love she gave to my brother.

Prior to my brother finding out he was HIV positive, he bought an insurance policy, $500,000 was to go to his wife, $500,000 to his children, and $500,000 to myself. I bought a house with the money I received. My parents moved in with me.

Rah, I love your show! Please continue to educate your viewers on how to love rather than hate, to value good people rather than being judgmental.

"People are angels and you don't realize he was an angel to his own father who didn't realize that because of his upbringing. He was not able to speak to his family and be truthful. rather than him keeping his secret which went so far, hurting everyone in the chain of lives, he touched deeply. Was it his fault or society and some of the bad teachings from the past?

Let's all think of his wife who knew all this and supported him by understanding him. That's true love and support by a person who was betrayed. As for his sister, she was the angel who never cast judgement but stood alongside him seeing his trust and love while returning that love and trust. be like this is life, be there for others, and don't try to judge them on things from the past. People do learn and people do change. sometimes it just takes some love and care."

YLEWRAH

FAMILY CHRISTMAS SPIRIT

Hello, it's the month of December and the Christmas spirit is in the air. Have you ever had a full blown over drive of the Christmas spirit? You know, shopping, catching up with friends, family and even colleagues about that jolly Christmas cheer.

My family is originally from New Jersey with a Caribbean mix of West Indian and Puerto Rican. Every Christmas my family and I would go to this beautiful cabin in Buffalo, NY. My dad had bought it for us. It was our home away from home. We loved celebrating Christmas together as a family there. It was our tradition. Even as my three sisters and I got older and had our own families, we kept the tradition going on.

My family loved celebrating Christmas! Three years ago it was a different kind of Christmas. We still got together to wrap the gifts, cook and decorate, etc. We always woke up and ate breakfast together. We would all exchange thoughts on how we felt about life and each other. We would tell each other what we meant to one another. However, on that Christmas morning no one could have predicted what events would have occurred.

Six months prior to Christmas I met this woman. She complained a lot, but was really sweet. In the few months we were together I noticed that anything she touched would fall apart so to speak. All of my family thought she was great and great for me except for my father. My dad was the type of person who just knew in his gut if people were good together or not. He felt that our spirits clashed in a bad way. Sometimes I thought it was just because my father didn't know how to handle me being a lesbian. Even though my father had doubts about my girlfriend, I continued to date her.

Christmas was now near and I told my girlfriend about my family tradition. She insisted on being invited so that she could share in the experience. I figured it would be ok to bring her as my brother-in-law had invited his sister this year. We all got to the cabin on Christmas Eve. We went out, bought a Christmas tree and brought it back to the cabin to decorate it together.

Around 1 p.m. on Christmas Eve, I was helping my dad and nephews put lights up around the front porch. My dad had asked me to run to the laundry room to get some tape. As I was about to open the laundry room door, I heard some loud noise and laughter. As I opened the door I saw my girlfriend with my brother-in-law's sister making out on top of the washing machine. I was in shock seeing what was going on. I must've let out a gasp, because all of a sudden they stopped and stared at me. Just as I was about to scream and demand what was going on, I heard my mother scream, "Fire, there's a fire!" I ran upstairs to see that our Christmas tree was in flames. My father quickly went to get the fire extinguisher and slowly put out the fire. There was smoke all over and everyone was horrified. Even though we put the fire out, there was still a lot of smoke around. My father inhaled a lot of smoke putting out the fire. It was too much for him and he fainted in front of all of us. My older sister quickly ran over to him and gave him CPR. Shortly after, the EMS got to the cabin and got my father into the ambulance. We got in our car to follow them to the hospital.

When we arrived at the hospital, my father was rushed to the ER. We waited for what seemed like a lifetime when one of his doctors came over to us. He told us that my father had suffered from a heart attack. When my mother heard this she fell to her knees in tears and screamed out with emotional pain for all of her daughters to surround her. As I was walking towards my mother I saw my girlfriend approaching me, reaching out her arms to hug me. Rather than embracing her hug, I just started to yell and scream at her. I screamed at her that my father's heart attack was all of her fault. I told her that all she brings is bad luck wherever she goes. I told her to get the 'F' away from me and my family and to get out of the hospital now! It took so much out of me emotionally to yell at her like that and at the same time deal with the news of my father suffering from a heart attack. As I watched her leave the hospital, I leaned on the wall, sliding down to the ground in tears.

I pulled myself up off the ground and wiped the tears from my eyes as I saw a doctor approaching my mother and sisters. I walked over to be with them. The doctor told us that my father was ok from the heart attack but suffering a bit from the smoke inhalation. The doctor explained that he wanted to observe him for a few hours and treat the smoke inhalation before he could release him from the hospital. The doctor said as long as all goes well, my father should be celebrating Christmas at home with his family.

My mother being who she is, gave everyone orders of what was needed for our Christmas morning together. The cabin needed to be cleaned, another Christmas tree needed to be purchased and decorated, the windows, even though it was cold, needed to be open to ventilate the cabin from the smoke, etc. The following morning we all were sitting around the table, including my father. My dad said that what made this Christmas morning more special because of the scare they all endured the night before.

My father went around the table telling all of us that in his sixty three years on this earth this was his happiest moment. He got a second chance, we all did. He told my mother how happy she had made him all of these years. She gave him four beautiful daughters while being an amazing wife, friend and partner to him. His speech brought tears to my eyes. I looked at my father and saw a very bright light above him which could only be described as the Christmas Spirit. It was a spirit of joy, peace and happiness. For that Christmas Spirit allowed my father to be with us for another Christmas breakfast. My father also went on to say that he noticed two guests that came to the cabin were no longer there. He looked at me and said I shouldn't worry. He told me my true love is on her way and to just be patient and hang on till she crosses my path.

My father passed away last summer. Sadly, I wasn't there because I was in Switzerland with my fiancé. Yes, my father was right and my true love found me and now we were engaged to be married. The Christmas after my father passed away was sad without him but we all kept up with our tradition. We all took turns talking about our favorite memories of him so that it was like he was still sitting with us around the breakfast table. He is now our Christmas Spirit.

Thank you, Rah, for Your Life Experiences with Rah. You have allowed people to share their stories which end up helping others. So keep up the good work, keep helping, keep motivating and keep inspiring.

Happy Holidays, Rah!

> *"Saying over and over again and again that everything happens in the right moment and at the right time is proven here. She found love and their family continued to show that same love they always do and kept their dad alive as his memory of all the amazing times they had with him never died. As for being betrayed and embarrassed all in one is no more proof that it was a blessing how everything happened and went in your life's love story at that time. You needed to learn and understand that betrayal to make you stronger and see everything happened at once. that they managed to still have an amazing christmas is really a test to remember in life. Hope this helps many who have been betrayed or embarrassed by the wrong person in one's life. Always be grateful for the amazing people who pull you up and hold you up when you are down - your amazing loving family and wonderful and meaningful friends in your life. Just as you look at all the negatives that you overcame in your life Always look out for the positives that you are surrounded with at times that overshadow the negatives. you just need to recognize and appreciate it."*

YLEWRAH

DANGEROUS GAME

Hey, Rah, thank you for your show "Your Life Experiences with Rah." Especially for Anonymous Monday's. I saw the episode about the guy who walked in on his mom who was bent over on her desk. When I saw that show I decided it was time to share my story. Well, to tell the truth, it's about a story I heard that I want to share with others. People need to know what happens when they take drugs and tell lies. I also hope that "Supergirl" is reading this. If you are, I would like to tell you how much I admire your family. I think the story I am about to tell will give you some competition.

So, the story I am about to share with you is about love and hate. The story was told to myself and nine others by a girl I will refer to as "Sandra". Sandra told us her story of how she used this guy to make him fall in love with her just so that she could get her citizenship in the USA. She ended up destroying his life and deporting him back from the US to his country. That was her plan from day one. Sad but true.

The man she tricked I will refer to as "Joey". Joey had been in a few failed relationships when he lived in his country. One day while he was at a religious function he met Sandra. Joey offered to have a long distance relationship since he was now living in the USA. Sandra agreed because in her head this was her ticket into the USA. So she made Joey believe that she was in love with him so that he would fall in love with her.

Joey planned on Sandra coming to the USA for a visit. While she was there she found out she was pregnant. She had an abortion and made Joey believe that she had a miscarriage. The truth was she wasn't even sure if the baby was Joey's. You see she was having an affair with another man back in her country. Joey had suspicions that she might have been seeing someone else. He confronted Sandra about it but she laughed it off and asked how he could think she would ever do anything that hurtful to him. So he shrugged it off since he was so madly in love with her.

As sweet as Joey was, he did have a temper. Sandra used that to her advantage. At times Joey would get so angry that he would be verbally abusive towards Sandra and would even break things in their house. Sandra would report this to the police as she was smart and building a case against him to frame him in the future.

So after a lot of smart planning, Sandra finally became a citizen of the USA. All the while she was still seeing the other man from her country. Time had passed and there was no more denying it to Joey. At this point she really didn't care anymore as she got out of Joey what she wanted. She was now a citizen and didn't need him anymore.

Once Sandra's citizenship went through, Joey had transferred the deed to his house 100 % to Sandra. For personal reasons he didn't want the house as an asset so he gifted it to Sandra. The mortgage was already paid in full, so she didn't have to worry about monthly payments. Shortly after that Sandra and Joey got into a major fight. Sandra left him and went to her ex who was now living in the US as well. Joey had gone over there to beg her to come home to him. What happened after that led to a court hearing.

While on trial, Sandra told her side of the story. In other words, she lied under oath to the judge, jury and everyone in the courtroom. She told everyone that Joey had been banging on the door loudly. When she opened the door he shoved her inside and grabbed her pushing her into the kitchen. There he found and picked up a knife. He held that knife to her throat and told her if she didn't come back home with him that he would kill herself and him. She went on to say that somehow she got out of his hold and ran to the bathroom. Once in there she locked the door so that Joey couldn't get in. He was banging on the door, threatening her to come out and if she didn't that he was going to kill himself. After about an hour she heard a weird noise. She waited a few moments before unlocking the bathroom door and going outside. She tip-toed into the kitchen where she found Joey unconscious, lying on the floor in a pool of his blood. She stood there in shock at first before calling 911.

Even though Joey didn't harm Sandra that day, the police had reports from Sandra about previous anger outrages. So he was charged with murder-suicide and was deported back to his country.

Joey didn't remember much of that night. He knew he was unconscious and was told that he had lost oxygen to his brain that led him into a coma for a few days Therefore, his memories from that night were all in a daze. He wasn't sure if what Sandra told the jury was true. Just that his gut told him something about her story was off.

The reason I and the nine other's know the truth is because Sandra told us the truth because she was high on drugs. We had all been at a party. Sandra smoked weed and did cocaine for the first time there. Therefore, she didn't hold back with any of the details. She confided that the reason she continued her relationship with her ex was because of the sex. Her ex would do things in bed that Joey didn't. She had been trying to leave Joey but he wouldn't let her go. That day when he came banging on the door she saw an opportunity. So yes, she opened the door and Joey grabbed her pushing her into the kitchen. However he didn't pick up the knife - she did. She turned and stabbed him. He was in shock so she knew she had to make her move. She pushed him which caused him to fall and hit his head leaving him unconscious. She kneeled down and stabbed him three more times. She stood there watching Joey in a pool of his own blood for an hour. She thought he was dead when she called 911. Till this day Sandra doesn't even recall telling us her story as she was so high and coked up that evening.

Sandra thought she could be with her ex freely now since Joey had been deported back to his country. However, her ex left her and married one of her close relatives back in their country. Joey was also doing just fine back home in his country. He made something of himself by opening up his own business. He was married and raising his six year old son.

Even though Sandra remained in the USA living in the house that Joey had gifted to her and was financially ok, mentally she wasn't. Every time she closed her eyes she would have nightmares of that night and the awfulness that she committed. I guess karma catches up with you.

So the moral of this story and why I shared it with you is to be careful of how you live your life. Treat others the way you would like to be treated. If you lie and do wrong to somebody, be ready to deal with the consequences.

"I just could never understand how some people can use another human being and betray them to this extent. This is sad and what makes it sad is how can you take an innocent person for granted with such a beautiful heart and break them like this. These people also know how to find your weak spots to prey upon, like his anger issues. Who knows? she may have brought up those anger issues along with dishonesty. people, don't hurt others today or tomorrow. It will come back. You might not understand at that moment you are in your glory but it does come back very badly. So many things happened in this story that can be explained but I love her ending and advice." (remember no real names were mentioned)

YLEWRAH

BETRAYAL WITH A PRICE

Where shall I start, Rah? Your show is amazing! My friends and I speak about it when we are having lunch together. Thanks to your show, it has given me the courage to share my story with you.

A little over eleven years ago I met this really handsome guy while I was attending Stoneybrook. It still amazes me when I think about how I still blush when I think of him. He makes me feel so good that it is like falling in love with him over and over each day that we are together. It was actually my husband who I am currently married to that pushed me to share my story with you. It was a major lesson that we both learned about trust actually as my story is his story.

So, like I began, we met a little over eleven years ago from today. A few months before we met, I had begun dating a man named Jake. Jake became his friend as well as mine. Jake was the type of guy that every girl or guy wanted by their side. Jake was a very intelligent man. He is now a cardiovascular surgeon. While we were dating, Jake would do anything to be with me. However, being with him came with a cost as he had another side to him. He lied to me in the nastiest of ways just to make me look bad so that he could look good to everyone else in our lives. I was very naive and would forgive him way too much as he would repeat this hurtful behavior during the whole time we were together.

The three of us actually ended up becoming really good friends. I didn't have any sexual feelings towards our new friend, so Jake didn't mind me having a male friend. He was always with us anyway, just in case. We would study together, go to parties together and eat out together. No, we never had a threesome. It was nothing like what happened in the "Supergirl" story. Our friends would see Jake's bad ways and let me know to be careful, but I still continued to overlook them. I assumed that Jake found out about this because if he saw me getting close with one of my girlfriends he would make up a lie about her and tell me that she wasn't good company for me. I was so blinded by my love for him, that I would believe his every word and stay away from that so-called friend or anyone else he told me not to get close to.

The semester is finally over. We all planned on heading home for the holidays. On our last night at college, I had plans to go out with some friends while my boyfriend and friend were heading to a party in the area. Something must've transpired between the two of them at that party because after that night everything changed.

You see I was very close to my friend I met a little over eleven years ago. I had a great platonic relationship with him. I was able to share everything with him and he was very easy to open up with. He also never bad mouthed Jake or my relationship with him. I never hid this from Jake and was thankful that he never told me not to hang out with my friend. I had no idea what was to come.

On our last night at the dorms, Jake came into my room in such a rage. He was cursing at me and calling me dirty things while smashing my room. I kept on asking what was wrong but he was so angry that he didn't answer me. He just kept yelling and screaming at me. It was the worst I ever saw him. I thought maybe he drank too much at the party or was on something, so I called my friend to see if he knew what was going on? However, when Jake saw that I was trying to call him he got even more angry and grabbed the phone out of my hand. He then threw my phone at the wall and broke it. Again, he started screaming: "How could I have done this to him"? He told me I disrespected our relationship and that I couldn't possibly love him since I betrayed him. I was still so confused. I had no idea what he was talking about, even though he was convinced that I was. I pleaded to him to just tell me what was wrong? He finally blurted out that I slept with my male friend. How could I betray him like that? How could I make him believe that we were just friends? I was shocked! I never lied to him. It was always him lying to me. Where did he hear this and why does he believe it? I tried to convince him that we never slept together. That I would never hurt him in that way. Jake being the very stubborn man he still didn't believe any of the words coming out of my mouth anymore. I knew I was just wasting my breath and Jake believed the worst of me. Jake just gave me a nasty look and left my dorm room.

I tried to fix my phone but couldn't. So I asked a friend if I could use her phone. I called my friend because where else would Jake have gotten this information except from him. However, he didn't answer his phone. So I decided to go to his apartment but there was no answer at the door. I thought maybe he headed home already. I kept on trying his phone for a few days and then got a notification that his phone had been disconnected.

A year had passed and, yes, I was still with Jake. We had even moved in together. Even though we were living together, Jake never let a day go without a daily reminder of how I had been unfaithful to him.

About two years ago I was at a medical conference in Pittsburgh. I was so concentrated on getting to my meeting on time that I didn't even see the person I bumped into. Everything I was carrying as well as the stranger's things that he was carrying fell onto the floor. As I leaned down to pick up my belongings while apologizing to the stranger, I heard a familiar voice. He said that nothing changed and that I was still as clumsy and beautiful as the last time he saw me. Was it really him? I stood up slowly to meet his eyes and all my feelings came rushing back. I still had a lot of hurt in me from this man. He embraced me with a hug when a flood of tears came rushing down my cheeks. I was filled with so many different emotions and didn't know what to do with them. I pushed him off of me as my conference was about to begin.

Now he was confused. He thought I would've been happier to see him. He wasn't letting me go. He followed me and called out my name to tell me to stop. I turned around and just yelled to him, "How could you?" "I trusted you." I never thought of you as a man who would betray our friendship. I thought you were different from Jake. I continued to tell him that I thought he was just a dirty sleaze ball and all I thought about the type of man he was was wrong.

He had this confused look on his face and at the same time a clarification popped up. He put two and two together about what had happened. He explained to me that Jake told him some things at that party they went to from the last night of college. Jake had told him that I said that he had been hitting on me and trying to get me into bed. Therefore, I didn't feel comfortable hanging out with him alone anymore. Jake had told him it was best that he take the job transfer as I never wanted to see him again. So now all these years, this man thought I hated him because of Jake's lies once again.

Rah, when I heard all of this, my eyes once again filled with tears. I asked my friend to please be honest with me. I asked him if he told Jake that we had slept together. I told him that was the lie Jake had told me on that last night and has held that lie over my head till this day. Now it was my friend's turn to have a flood of emotions as his eyes were filled with tears. That's how I knew we had both been played by a jealous self-centered pig like Jake. This time we held each other while apologizing over and over to one another.

My friend went on to tell me that he needed to confirm all that Jake had told him on that night. However, each time he called me it went straight to voicemail. I explained that Jake had broken my phone that night after I had tried to call him. I needed to go into my meeting so I asked him for his current phone number and told him I would call as soon as my meeting was over.

I kept my promise and called my friend once my meeting let out. We went to my hotel room to call Jake and confront him together. I asked Jake to meet me at my hotel room. When he walked in, a look of shock was on his face. I smiled and said look who I ran into before my meeting earlier. Now Jake had a look of oh what the F is going on here? I walked over to my friend very slowly as I started to undress myself. At this point even my friend was confused as to what I was doing. I didn't care, I needed to get back at Jake in the only way I knew would hurt him. I started to kiss my friend very passionately. This of course made Jake livid. My friend was too good of a man and stopped it from going any further at that point. I finally had the strength to walk away and leave Jake that day. That lie that he made up to both of us was like a dark cloud over both of our heads for years. Discovering it was all a lie removed any love I had for Jake that day. I left and never looked back.

Another fantastic thing happened on that day. I realized I had all these feelings for my friend that I never knew I had in the past. I never allowed myself to go there because of my respect for Jake. After that kiss in the hotel room, there was no denying all those feelings. Luckily, he felt the same way. It has been ten months now since we got married and both of us couldn't be happier. He makes me feel like I fall in love with him over and over each day we wake up next to each other.

Thank you, Rah, for Your Life Experiences with Rah. I hope my story can help others to learn a lesson about trust, love and betrayal. If you are questioning the person you are in love with, then most likely that is the wrong person for you. If someone makes an accusation, get confirmation from the other person's mouth before believing what you hear. Life is precious and as we all know tomorrow is not promised, so make sure you spend it with someone who makes you fall in love with him or her day after day.

"Everything was just said so nicely at the end."
YLEWRAH

ANGELS DO EXIST

Hello, Rah, I just want to let you know that you are doing such wonderful things on your show "Your Life Experiences with Rah." My story is not a lengthy one, but I do want to send a message out there to the young ladies. I want ladies to have a voice as it is their right living in America.

A while back I met a girl from my building who was crying on the staircase. I sat down next to her so she had someone to talk to. She told me she has so many bills to pay and is out of work and doesn't know what to do. You know, Rah, the everyday story of how people like you and I struggle on a day to day basis due to finances. I spoke with my manager at work later that week to see if there were any openings. There were and so I had her come in and talk with my manager to see if she was a good fit. Luckily, she was.

Since we were now working together, we were seeing each other on a daily basis. She was now comfortable enough to open up to me about her situation. She told me that her family moved to America from Jamaica and how her mother met her stepfather. She told me how her stepfather would rape her night after night. When she finally got the emotional strength to tell her mother about what was going on, she got mad at her and accused her of making the whole thing up for attention. Once she was eighteen she ran away from home and got a place in my apartment building.

She continued to tell me her story. Not only did her stepfather rape her at the early age of thirteen, she also got pregnant as a result of the rape. When her stepfather found out about the pregnancy, he kicked her in the stomach to get rid of the baby. He continued to rape her and she continued to get pregnant as a result of the rapes. Her stepfather would either get her to have an abortion or he would personally take care of the problem.

A few days after she started working at my office, she came in with cramps. I told her she should see a doctor. As the day went on, her cramping got worse and she fainted. That is when I called 911. I was able to go in the ambulance with her to the hospital. When we got to the hospital, she asked if I was able to stay with her as I was the closest thing to family. So they allowed me to stay with her.

The doctors at the hospital did some tests and found out she had some internal damage and bleeding. She was admitted to the hospital for treatment for a few days before she was discharged. I made sure to take care of her. My son and I would take her out to dinner a few nights a week to make sure she was ok. We would go to her apartment to keep her company as well. One evening she told me she got me something. It was a beautiful picture frame of us. She thanked me for all I had done for her and said I was her angel. She then hugged me and broke out in tears. She was so filled with emotion. She told me that no one has ever shown her the love, care and generosity that I had. She told me that she didn't want to worry me that she was diagnosed with stage 4 uterine cancer and had about five more years before she would leave this Earth to be my angel.

I tried my best to comfort her and tell her not to worry. I told her we would get through it together. She just curled into my arms and cried. I couldn't sleep that night. This woman was not twenty years old and didn't deserve this fate. I prayed to Jesus for a miracle.

A few evenings later, she committed suicide. She swallowed all of her pain pills and her heart failed. Rah, she left me a note. It read, "My angel. They always said that angels exist and I only really found this out when you stepped into my life that day on the staircase. I really saw a bright light in you. I don't ever want you to feel that you failed me or that you could have done more for me. You did everything you could've done for me and I wanted you to know that I appreciated all of it. You showed me and made me understand what love felt like and what it truly is. I am sorry to have to do this and to leave you. I ask for one more thing from you in order to keep my memory alive. Tell parents to believe in their children, even when the kids tell you the unthinkable has happened."

Rah, I'm still heartbroken by this loss but I saw your show and knew it was the right opportunity to share this so the world can hear my story and learn from it.

"Today I read on this "pastor's" post on facebook his ranting and raving about witchcraft and who is trying to hurt him and his family, even going further to use the book of psalms to help keep the demons out. I am sure and very sure he knows about stories like this. How does he comfort these people by speaking about the evil that occurred thousands of years ago? This evil exists in human beings, not demons. a man's (human) mind is the most powerful thing, and how he is groomed is how it is shaped. a man's brain is also damaged by the types of betrayal we have heard. How is witchcraft and speaking about other humans, using the bible and different spiritual ways, helping those that follow him with mental health issues? Religion is there to keep you and guide you from going off the path of righteousness but it doesn't teach you how to handle the mental stress some go into or go through when life traumas happen. it teaches you to pray, which is a great thing: your mind will feel better. But, at the end of the day, the person who does most of the miracles is you to get you where you need to go and be in your life, running far away from those that cause the main mental problems of life that are not necessary. Keep loving yourself and believing in yourself. If God has created you in his image, you want to make sure you are a god in your life and love you the way you should be loved. I love you, and you are essential. keep believing as rah believes in you all. the following story you all will love as it definitely will help you to "believe"."

YLEWRAH

NEVER ASK FOR TOO MUCH

Hey, RAH, I'm from Virginia. I came across your show recently. A friend shared your story "an angel was born" people listen to other people's stories and say it sounds like a movie at times. Most people use the phrase "I could write a book about my life" without a doubt that is so true. What is also true is your life is not that unique because what you think you have accomplished in life, someone has done beyond, whatever dangerous paths you may have thought you alone have walked on, others have done worse. You are such an angel yourself to take time off to share the life stories of others to help those that need to know to wake up. It's not just you facing this, not just someone, but many others have been where you are, and they have gotten past it. Love how you tell your viewers to wake up, shake off, take a deep breath, tell yourself I love you, and reach for their goals.

My story is similar to "An angel has been born." I met my first husband in high school. We dated, even when we were separated by different colleges, we somehow managed to keep our relationship strong.

You know, maintaining love is not an easy task. I have learned that it's so easy to get distracted by lust, especially in these modern times.

It won't wait till our 4th year of marriage that a woman showed up with a 5-year-old child and claimed it was my husband's son as they were college sweethearts. We have been trying to have a baby since we got married, but it just never happened.

Now he said she was lying and he didn't want to be with her. He is married to me blah blah blah. It went on and on for a few days like that. Until he came saying he wanted to get to know his son. I didn't have a problem with that. Within a few months, he asked me for a divorce. Yes, that's what happened. He remarried his son's mother. 3 years later, he had some sort of complications and passed away.

It took me about 4 years to really trust another. After my marriage broke like that, I didn't feel the need to be with any man or be hurt again because I was afraid I would never be fixed.

My company merged with another giant company. While overlooking some plans, someone from the new company had to check up to see how our clients' projects were coming in.

He was on his way back to me and said, "Has anyone told you how sad you look? I didn't even look at him while he was there until that moment I looked up and saw this guy. I felt a connection to him like somehow I knew him from somewhere ever got that feeling rah, that there is some reason he was sent. Won't too long after, he came by my office to apologize for what he said and to make it up wanted to take me to lunch. I agreed.

Lunch was downtown. While driving, we got into an accident. I woke up in the hospital to find out I had some complications with my womb and might never become pregnant.

My husband, to this day, thinks everything is his fault. He blames himself for everything that happened, which was nothing to point fighters at him for. The accident was a man who got a heart attack behind his wheel and the other part you are about to hear. After the accident, I tried to stay away from him, but he felt it was his fault for always buying me flowers, stuffed animals, and jewelry which I would refuse. We kept seeing each other until he asked me to marry him. Saying 'No' was like saying propose me again tomorrow because I think he asked me every day for at least 6 months before I gave in.

Not to be harsh, don't judge me, but he won't be the type of guy every girl will look back at twice. Now, this doesn't mean that he won't cheat because I have seen it happen with my girlfriends and their cheating lying ass bfs.

We started Our journey to start a family knowing it might never happen, but not giving up seeing different ob gyns and specialists to make this happen. 3 years after taking other meds and trying different techniques, I got really depressed. I stopped working, started resenting my husband, started blaming this sweet man who never stopped saying sorry about the accident. I pushed away my family. All I wanted by then was to have a baby.

I decided I didn't want to see another doctor. It's over; it's not happening. Got me back together headed back to work. Sat my husband down and asked him to tell me clearly if he was ok if we couldn't have children. I showed him my point as to why I believe we should not adopt. If it was meant for us to have a baby, we would have one on our own. He turned to me and said, "I fell in love with you; I married you. I don't plan on going anywhere. You are my everything. I would love to have kids and a family but not doing any of that without you. Always remember it only happens in the right moment at the right time. I love you."

We lived our lives as usual until our 5th anniversary my husband took me to New Orleans. On the streets, one night, a strange gypsy-looking woman ran behind me out her hands on my belly and said to me, being blessed is a curse and will bring pain to you. Get rid of him now. Don't get attached. My husband pushed her off as she continued to ramble as we walked off. 2 weeks later, I found out I was 7 weeks pregnant.

I remember this moment till this day, I'm not a believer in god, but I know it was a miracle. Not too long after, Tyler came into our lives. Rah, I couldn't have been happier. I saw my husband so glad I just looked at him with our baby, knowing this has really made him happy the way he makes me feel satisfied.

We gave our son so much love and care. Until that day when we both were on our way to a good friend's birthday party, it was only 3 months to Tyler's 6th birthday. Never forget this day, as it was Good Friday. While waiting at the traffic light, there was a massive noise with a slam that sent our car spinning into the middle of the intersection into the pathway of an oncoming vehicle that came slamming and impacting my little car on the same side as my baby in the back.

Everything came to a crashing stop. People scrambling out of their cars, I somehow got out of the car, rushing to get Tyler out. I stood there watching as another car was on top of the side of my car where Tyler was. I started to scream as I tried to get him out. Others came to assist. We couldn't and had to wait for the EMS to save my baby. You will never know until you are in this situation. It felt as though time just kept going, and my child was dying or in pain. Finally, after it seemed like hours in a few minutes, the EMS was there. I stood there watching as they removed my precious baby covered in blood.

I have been through many different interviews after this happened, and every time I tell this story, I still cry. He was pronounced dead in the ER.

As much as this is heartbreaking, I forgot to mention I never told any of the reporters this part of my story, I really love what you are doing, and I must share it with you and your followers. His words to me moments before the accident. Tyler said, "Mummy, I'm going away but remember mummy, I will be back, and I love you, mummy." I was so confused as to what this little guy was saying to me, but that moment after breaking down next to him in the ER, I heard his voice repeating it as clear as day.

It wasn't one year later. I had another baby boy this time. He was born on Easter Monday, yes RAH, I don't know who God is. I'm not a hypocrite that something changed or happened well, and I will seek out something I don't know of. I trust everything which has blessed me and is always there for me and my family.

Rah, when my son was 8 years old, we were approaching that very same intersection all of a sudden. He screamed out, "Mummy, nooooo, please don't stop, don't stop. My other 2 daughters in the car got really scared. I pulled over and opened the back door, hugging him, saying Tyler, mummy is here, nothing will happen to you, with tears in his eyes, he looked at me and said, "Mummy, I told you I would be back." As his head went backward while my daughters and I screamed his name, he immediately jumped, asking us what's the matter. I looked at him with tears in my eyes as I knew that he was really my Tyler. Rah, the thing is, my son's name is Connor. He's a young man now about to be a father for the first time. I like how you always speak of this supreme looking over us, a really nice way to put it, and you don't have to follow any sort of religious beliefs.

Rah, don't you ever stop this motivating and inspiring by allowing others to share their stories.

> *"I wanted this story to be added to help lots of you to believe more. Don't stop believing regardless of what you believe in. Remember, keep thinking positive, and the positives will happen. just believe."*
>
> YLEWRAH

FAT SWEET BOTTOM

Rah, after I heard about your abuse by your stepfather, I knew I had to share my story. I want to help everyone to know that even when we feel we are alone, we are not. Thanks To Your Life Experiences with Rah, it allows us to open up and help those who feel they are going through similar issues alone. I am gay as well as everyone will hear in my story. I always knew from a young age I was attracted to men but I kept it to myself, always.

I am too not looking for sympathy for my story. However, when you talk about a mother abandoning her son that brought up my living situation in some ways. I don't blame my mother. After hearing my story, you all can make the decision if you would've blamed her.

When I was almost fourteen, my mother left my abusive father with my little sister who was nine at that time. It's sad to know they are both in a good place in life and I have no grievances towards my mother or my sister. They don't have much of a role in my life today. My father has one leg and is partially blind with diabetes. That is what I hear about him anyway.

One night after my mother left, my father and his friends came home drunk. Later on two of them went home, while my father and his other friend that he was very close to were still drinking. As I was walking by where my father and his friend were drinking, I overheard my father's friend say to him, "Your son has a nicer bottom than my wife!" My father's friend said, "I don't have money on me right now, but I have a bottle of Johnny Walker back in the car. I will give it to you as payment so that I can feel how that fat bottom of your son's feels." My father told his friend to get the bottle of Johnny Walker and then he can have sex with his son. My father sold me for a bottle of Rum Rah! When I heard him say that, I was shocked! I yelled don't come near me or I will run away from here tonight.

Rah, my father grabbed me and held on to me so that I couldn't run. I even tried to bite him, but he threw me to the floor. Then his friend walked in and my father took that bottle from him and walked into the other room. His friend locked the door behind him and raped me! My father knew his friend was going to rape me and not only allowed it to happen, but heard my screams from the other room and never stopped it! I will never forget this day as it both broke me as well as made me who I am today.

I also remember the exact time this happened to me. It was 10:52 p.m. He looked at me saying he would be gentle. He turned me around and pulled down my shorts, spit on his fingers and with his giant gorilla looking fingers he started pushing them inside of me. He lied. It was the opposite of gentle, it was brutally rough. I was in extreme pain, something I don't know how to explain. I begged him to stop. He pulled his fingers out quickly and roughly making it more painful. He then pushed me to the floor and pulled out his dirty ugly penis before entering me as I screamed out so loud. Then I passed out from the pain as well as the nightmare that didn't seem real, but it was. I regained consciousness when he was about to finish. He was going in and out of me squeezing me to the floor as I felt pain all over. Finally he made a loud noise and just stayed on top of me like that for about two minutes.

I didn't move, I just felt tears flowing from my eyes down my cheeks in complete shock of what just happened to me. When he finally got off of me I struggled to get off the floor but I remembered looking at the clock and it was 10:58 p.m. It felt like the longest six minutes of my life! I struggled to walk to the toilet as I felt I needed to go. There was a lot of blood and stool that was all mixed up from the torture that I had just went through. I will never forget this day. I heard my father in a drunken state say to his friend, "Did you enjoy him?" His friend just left without answering him.

My father woke up the next morning like nothing had happened. I didn't know what to do. I felt alone in this world. My mother had abandoned me, left without knowing where she went. I left for school but I never ended up there. I was in too much pain, emotionally as well as physically. There was an abandoned house not too far from my school where kids went to play sometimes. I cried a lot that day as I felt so lost. So many thoughts went through my mind. When I got back home my father still acted like nothing had happened. I hated my father but had nowhere to go.

Even though I had already known that I liked the same sex, the thought of a man touching me was too much to bare. A month had passed by and one day on my way home from school a car pulled up to me. My heart stopped, it was him! He wanted me to get into his car, but I kept on refusing. So he says to me, "If you do not get into the car, I will have to tell your father about you disrespecting me. Is that something you want?" I didn't want any trouble with my father, so I got into the car. He drove off to a secluded area in the woods and parked. He then turned to me and said, "Please don't be afraid of me, I just want to talk with you. I just want to tell you that I am sorry for the other night. I was drunk out of my mind and I'm sorry if I hurt you." He continued to tell me that every time I would walk by him he would get turned on by me. He offered to give me money if I agreed to him having sex with me each time. Only if I allowed him to do whatever he wanted to do to me. He even went as far to tell me that he promised if I told him to stop he would because he didn't want to hurt me again. He went further to tell me that he wouldn't touch me right now and that he would take me home. He said that only to gain my trust, which he did. As he pulled up to my house, my father was outside watching me get out of his car. As of now almost thirty-two year old gay man, I constantly think how could any adult look at a child as a sex figure? I was too young to comprehend it when it was happening to me, because after all I was just a child. As an adult I still cannot comprehend this because I can never look at any child and have the thoughts and feelings that this man had for me.

It took me becoming an adult to understand that that man was not mentally stable, something a thirteen year old cannot make sense of. Getting back to the story. My father asked me where I was all this time and why did it take me two hours longer to get home? Before I was even given the chance to tell him the truth, he slapped me and slapped me so hard that I fell to the floor.

As I was getting up he kicked me as I hit the bed. He held me down with his foot so I couldn't move. I turned my head to see what he was doing and I saw him pulling his broad leather belt out his pants. The same one he used to beat my mother with. He pulled my pants down to my ankles as I screamed to the top of my voice begging him to stop and I would tell him the truth.

Before I could say anything more I started feeling the lashes on my bottom and I screamed and screamed begging him to stop. But he didn't. I could see him hitting me mercilessly on my lower back and bottom. I don't know if I went into shock or what but I was not feeling anything anymore and it all went numb. I think I got about thirty lashes with that belt, maybe more? When he finished beating me he grabbed me by the back of my neck and slammed me to the floor kicking me and calling me nasty names. When I started to scream for him to stop he gave me one final kick and walked out the room.

I laid on the floor crying until I fell asleep or went unconscious, I don't know? I remember waking up the next morning in so much pain. My father was not home because he had gone to work.

When I looked in the mirror there were dried up blood marks in colors of blue and black. I didn't know what to do or where to turn. I had no mother and a devil for a father. My grandparents on both sides were dead. Nowhere to turn. All I thought about was to go to my uncle's, my father's older brother's house to tell him what was going on. My uncle wasn't home anyway. He and his family had gone to America for vacation as their son was studying in Florida. It would be another three weeks before they would be back.

I didn't go to school that week. I couldn't sleep. I couldn't sit and no one knew the pain I was going through. I am not even sure if this man knew what he did to me to this day?

Three weeks felt like three years. Finally my aunt and uncle had come back from their vacation. I went to their house and told them everything. They left me in the living room and went to the kitchen where I could hear them talking and I did hear my uncle say that he didn't want a faggot living in his house. My aunt told him to have a heart, let's take him back and find out the truth. I begged them not to take me home, but they did. When we got to my father's house he was almost drunk which was just a regular day for me.

He gave them his own version of the story. That his friend was there and I sat on his friend's lap with my own free will and rubbed my bottom on his friend's penis. That's why he gave me a beating, because he didn't raise a faggot. I started to cry telling them that he was lying. I ran and I held on to my aunt's feet as I begged her to take me and not leave me there. My cousin who was my age said to her mother let's take him and not leave him in that house. My aunt said to my father don't ever come around him ever or come to my house or I will go to the police. I looked up and I swear I didn't see my aunt, but the image of God.

I got whatever clothes I had and went to live with them. They never asked me for anything. They took care of me like I was one of their own. But everyone in Florida knew the story and at times I was not sure if they believed me or my father? I guess those scars helped me?

About a year and half later their son who was about twenty-three came back from Florida as he had very bad stomach problems. I had been living in his room, but now that he was back we had to share his room or I had to live in the living room. (Note: my cousin became my first love)

My cousin, my prince, the first man I ever fell in love with. How I could never forget that day we went to pick him up at the airport. The photos at the house my family had of him didn't do justice. Lean 6' male looking model. I was in awe of him.

Rah, you're gay and I'm sure you can relate to this. When you get a look from a man and you just know something is up? That was how I felt when I saw him for the first time. We got home and he went straight to his room. I asked him if he would like me to get my things out of his room. He told me that we could share his room because I wasn't that big, the only thing that was, was my butt!. I must admit I blushed and walked out the room. Within a month we were like best buddies. It was a couple of months from my sixteenth birthday and I was excited just to be around him. We would drive all over the place and he loved to speed which was a rush for me. My first drink of alcohol was given to me by him and another one of his old classmates. Can you guess what my first drink was? Oh yeah a shot of Johnny Walker. Till this day it remains one of my best drinks, I love it straight up on the rocks. I guess it's me taking back my power from that man tried to rape me off?

One day about two weeks before my sixteenth birthday, the craziest thing happened. My cousin told me that he needed a favor and if I agreed, he would give me whatever I wanted for my birthday. I asked for his denim jacket even though it was much bigger on me. Just having it and being able to smell him is all I wanted. He agreed. The favor he wanted from me was to wear three different pairs of women's panties. He just wanted to take pictures of me in these panties to show his friends and lie to them that it was of some chick he was having sex with. Stupid me I agreed.

That night he came home drunk. I was in bed. Normally he never tried to wake me or make noise, but that night I heard him. I woke up without him realizing I was awake. I peeked at him as he got naked. He got into bed with me, yet he had never slept next to me without his clothes on. Rah, he kept moving and turning in the bed until he finally put his foot over my legs. I didn't move. I was excited, happy and scared all in one. He slowly pulled the sheet off that I was covered with and then he took his fingers and gently stroked them up and down my back. He came up closer to me and whispered asking me if I was awake? I was not sure how to answer but I nodded yes. He said everyone was talking about me not knowing whose photo it was. I got mad and horny at the same time wanting you, I just wanted to come home and get on top of you. Then he said don't be afraid I won't do something to hurt you and won't if you don't want to. He started kissing my ears and back as he turned me over and pressed his huge body on me and started making out with me. I will never forget this night as long as I live. It was everything I had dreamed of happening. To my surprise the next morning he woke up telling me not to ever let his parents or anyone know about this. He asked me if I wanted to do it again and before I could reply he was all over me once again. This went on like that every night and before I could reply he was all over me once again. This went on like that every night and every spare minute we would have which was very exciting. I was living the happiest time of my sixteen year old life!

A few weeks later he took me to a party. It was his friend's uncle's birthday as well as mine. When we got there everyone looked at me funny. I met all of his friends, who were all males. The weird thing was that his friend's uncle wasn't there. It was weird because the party was to celebrate him and he wasn't there.

A lot of heavy drinking went on for a few hours and then one of the guys pulled out a bag of rocks and started crushing it. Yep, it was cocaine. They all started to sniff it, including my new lover, my cousin. They then started forcing me to do it as well even though I tried convincing them that I didn't want any.

When they got high my cousin announced to everyone that he had something to say. He looked at me and called me to stand beside him. At this point I was thinking all sorts of things. Is he really about to tell everyone we are an item and having sex? But he said turn around and show the guys the secret.

I tried to ask him what he was talking about, but he grabbed me and spun me so quickly and roughly while he pulled my pants down. He then turned to his friends and said this is that sweet fat bottom I showed you all - it's not a woman. I enjoyed him in every way and now as a birthday present to him, I want you all to have a turn with him. I promise you will enjoy him. I was shocked! Was he joking? I started to pull my pants up and said that it wasn't going to happen and turned to leave. My cousin wasn't allowing it. He grabbed a handful of the cocaine and I had no choice but to inhale it. Everything started to spin. Two of the guys started to take mine and their clothes off. I was trying not to allow this to happen, but my mind was spinning and I had no control over my own body. All I could see in a blurred state was one of the guys bending me over onto the sofa as he took more cocaine and stuck it inside of me.

One by one, they all had their way with me and as much as I wanted and tried, I couldn't move and had to let it happen.

Rah, everyone has some type of sleep paralysis. Mine is all of the nightmares that were actual reality. No matter where I turned, men thought it was ok to rape me over and over again. I feel like evil and the devil chased me wherever I turned and therefore my sleep got interrupted time and time again. About two months ago I had a nightmare of what had happened at that party. It's like I died and my soul was watching a replay of this. I could see what was going on and yet again, I couldn't move. Rah, these guys were just having their way with me. Even though I was screaming, it wouldn't stop. I would think it was over and then another guy came and tortured me, sometimes worse than the one before him. If that was even possible. This horrible nightmare which was my reality carried on for an hour and half. Not six little minutes, an hour and a half! I thought the torture was finally over when the front door opened and there with blue eyes meeting mine I see the man who first tortured me like this. My past was back again.

To my surprise, he was actually appalled by what he saw going on in his living room and told everyone to STOP! I heard one of the guys that raped me tell my past, "C'mon, you're just in time to get in on the action. The three of us just came really good to him." My past just looked.

My cousin heard this and slapped the guy who just said those hurtful things. I'm hearing all of these things and feeling that my body is still numb from what just happened as well as from the cocaine that was also forced into me. I wanted to vomit, but couldn't.

I remember my father's friend, my past was washing my face while my cousin watched as he tried to help. Together they got me into my cousin's car. As bad as it was, my cousin got me back home and tucked me into bed so that I could go to sleep. As he tucked me in, he whispered into my ear, "I'm really sorry about what happened and even worse, that I allowed it to."

He did say to me if I told anyone at home where we went and what had happened that he will tell his parents I'm a faggot. Don't forget, my father hates faggots.

The next morning when I awoke, I saw my cousin just staring at me. He told me he was very worried about me. That all night, all he saw were the visions of what had happened to me and how very sorry he was. I guess the guilt was kicking in? Or so I thought, because he then started to touch me but I pulled away and told him to never touch me again!

A few days later I knew I couldn't share a room with my cousin anymore, let alone sleep on the same bed with him. So I asked my aunt if I could sleep on the couch in the living room and I would make sure to wake up before everyone else so they could have access to that room. She asked me why? What had happened that I no longer wanted to share a room with her son? Does he snore too loud or did you guys get into a fight? Then she told me it wasn't any of her business and that if I wanted to sleep in the living room that I could. She told me that it was my house as well. Before she turned to walk away, I asked her if she needed any help attending to the pigs that she and my uncle take care of. She turned to me and pulled me into her arms, giving me something I didn't even realize how much I desired. She hugged me. I don't remember the last time I felt love, like I did in that hug. She asked what had gotten into me? She told me that she loves me as much as she loves her own children. That I am her third child ever since they took me under their wings. She then said if my two children do not help out with the pigs, why do you think you should? I just held onto her so tightly. I didn't want to let go. I was afraid to let go. That hug reminded me that even after all the horrible torture I have experienced, that I am still important in someone's eyes and that I am loved. I just looked into her eyes and thanked her and told her that she will always have a special place in my heart.

A few weeks later I was home with my cousin only. He came into the living room telling me how much he loved me and that I am all that he thinks of. He went on to tell me his heart is breaking because I wasn't talking to him and he needs me to talk to him and needs me to love him back. He told me if I didn't love him back that he was going to kill himself.

Rah, I'm not sure where I got the strength from but I just pushed him away just as he was leaning in to kiss me. I turned to him and told him that if he ever approached me again, I would tell his parents and everyone he knows that he's a faggot and about what he allowed his friends to do to me, one by one. He was crying at that point, telling me he was going to kill himself. I looked at him and told him to go ahead and do it! I fell in love with you. You made me believe there was good in the world again. I thought I could count on you and trust you. I never thought you would take my youth away or hurt me in the way you did that night. I am only sixteen. I shouldn't know a world that I now know because of that night. I will never allow myself to trust again. I will always have my walls up, because I will never allow what happened that night to ever happen to me again! You destroyed me!

As it turns out, I never did allow myself to love or trust another person, at least not in the way I loved my cousin. My cousin continued to try to get my forgiveness, but I couldn't even endure see him. I guess his guilt turned into anger, because he tried sending me back to my mother, but his mother said that wasn't possible as my mother was still having issues. A few months later he drank poison and killed himself. I know I should've felt some kind of remorse, but unless what happened to me happened to you… you will never understand. He was a monster, a part of the devil in my eyes. He broke my heart and shattered me into pieces that could never get put back together again.

People speak about forgive and forget, Rah. Can you or anyone forgive someone who did that to you? Forgetting all that happened and still loving them? Maybe? I just couldn't. Does that not make me strong? Maybe, I know I felt broken. I didn't know how to repair myself. Maybe if I was able to, I could've forgiven him? That is something I will never know but I am ok with that. If that makes me a bad person, so be it. I'd rather be considered a bad person for not knowing how to forgive rather than being the type of people like my assaulters. Wouldn't you agree?

Rah, I know there are other stories out there worse than mine and that everyone deals with it in different ways. I share my story because of you and what your show has allowed me to realize about those types of people. They hurt us and make us feel like there is something wrong with us, otherwise this wouldn't have happened to me. Your show teaches us that isn't true. Through your show, we will all realize we aren't alone. We can talk and share and by doing so, little by little, we will be able to sleep more and more without the nightmares waking us up.

I shouldn't feel ashamed of the horrible things that happened to me. They happened to me, I didn't ask for them to happen. So why do I feel ashamed? That is the power of those people. They take away our worth. Your show teaches us not to be ashamed. That it wasn't our fault. Also, that we aren't alone.

"It takes a strong person to really go through all this and keep standing. You see, in 2015, I went through a hell of a bad time where I felt that the challenges of life were too much and I felt like not living anymore. I got out of it and I will tell you all how. The last story you will read is regarding my abusive step father. I wanted you to know you are not alone and Rah went through this with you all in a different way or many different ways during my life as you all will read in "rah's story".

My current stepfather, who is an amazing man, is the father I would have loved to really be born to. but i didn't have to be born to him. he has shown me love and care by being there for me in my darkest times and i'm grateful for the man he is. he said to me last year (2020) one day as he saw me after raising up the ashes 5 years later: "Rah, you know what happened to you? you are always ready for life. you were always ready to swing that bat and slam the life ball straight on because it's who you are. you are ready for life's challenges, but this time life decided you are too good. even against the best fastballs that would have gone your way, you know how to smack them dead on. life decided to hit you with a curve ball and that ball blindsided you and you just didn't expect it. It was like a ghost from the past. you thought you would never resurface in a different way and you just couldn't manage to hit that slam you normally do." it made so much sense - his explanation of life throwing you a curveball.

What I did was tell myself I want to see what's next and I decided to smile. on the 31st of december 2015, i said: "tomorrow i will wake up and love myself as i need me to be ok and never be in the place i was in the past year. I need myself to smile and face everyday, rising up towards the challenges and expecting anything from anywhere from anyone in life. I did that and when january of 2016 came and the same problems were there, I was less stressed. By April of that year, when I look back, things started getting much better and started falling into place. I started believing more and more that the more positive you are and think, the more smiles and easier challenges life sends your way. (trust me it's the same harder and harder challenges but just that you are in a stronger place to handle them as they come to you). continue to believe everything is going to be ok and believe in yourself. Never stop loving yourself and put yourself first in a good way and not a selfish one.

Let's love and share the love we want in return. As I always say: "where is the time to hate when there is so little time to love?"

Rah loves you all.

YLEWRAH

YOUR LIFE EXPERIENCES WITH RAH

PHYSICALLY ABUSED BY A LOVED ONE

I want to share my story of Physical Abuse with you all.

My parents divorced each other when I was barely eighteen months old. I don't have any memories of my biological father.

Therefore, I do not know the true love of what it feels like to be loved by a father.

I saw what it should be like from seeing the relationship between my cousins and uncles and my friends and their fathers.

Later on, my mother was in a new relationship, and I got a stepfather. He was the only father I knew, and therefore, I started calling him daddy.

However, this man that I considered my father repeatedly beat me, which caused a lot of bruises to my body. I never understood why he did that to me? What did I do to make my father hate me? Why didn't my daddy love me?

Not only was my stepfather physically abusive, but he was verbally abusive as well.

One memory I have had with my cousin when we were children. My cousin would run around the house in nothing but a T-shirt and a pair of underwear. Since she was a young child at that time, there was nothing really inappropriate about it. My stepfather, of course, turned it into something that it really wasn't. He would grab my young cousin and put his hand on her waist while slightly touching her underwear and then have her face me. He would tell her to show me what her (in Trinidadian language "CUNT") vagina looked like!

Another horrible memory I have of him is when he beat me up with a wooden broom. He acted as if he hadn't done anything or hurt me, but by the time he was done brutally beating me, the broom had broken into four different pieces.

Once, he tried to lay a hand on my mother instead of me. That was the day when I stood up to him and he ran me out the house with a machete. I never stepped foot back in his house as I had to leave and go live with my grandmother.

Years later, my mother and I left Trinidad and moved to America.

Somehow this man found us and got our number. He called us and left a very threatening voicemail. He told us that he had a gun and when he found us, he would kill us. We reported him to the police; they tracked him down and arrested him.

Up until a few years ago I still had nightmares about this. Yes, it was long ago, but I still dreamt about him and I was always fighting.

I wanted to share my story with all of you so that you know that you are not alone. No one should ever experience this kind of abuse. This isn't love.

If you are going through something like this and can get out - *"Get out while you can!"*

Thank you to all my friends and family who have supported me throughout the years. You have helped me overcome the nightmares and become the person I am today.

> *"Many times, you ask yourself how a person can become the way my stepfather was in this story I shared. Is it society, family, culture, upbringing or alcohol abuse? To be honest, as I said in the story, I knew him as my father and he would be one of the sweetest, caring, loving people that you could wish for. He would always be like that. Now, on the other hand, mental health is such a huge issue as we know and once again I will call it out. (I'm not blaming everything on this because you have a mind of your own and can judge and assess a situation as well as know that a relationship is built on trust.)*
>
> *Let's say my stepfather was obsessed with my mom, a good and beautiful woman. She then leaves her husband and she ends up with you with a child. family members would say to*

him: "if she did that to her husband why won't she do it to you?" That's the first seed planted of negative thoughts that will never leave the echoes of his mind. Then you had friends and others telling you about the beautiful sexy woman he had. Another seed is thereby planted by him thinking that since she is beautiful and sexy, why wouldn't she cheat on him - which stays with him and throughout the years will manifest into thoughts that were not true. but for him, it was all true in his mind. his alcohol abuse and his stalking of my mother anywhere she worked - not even working at times himself. Well, he would usually always lose his job after staying away for long periods when he went to drink. There were times I came from school and found my mom beaten up because she would try to speak to him about cutting work and coming home with friends while being already halfway drunk. On many nights at many different early hours of the morning, we would have to run out of the house and go to my other uncle and aunt's house who lived not too far away as he wanted to beat my mom and wanted to kill her. Not to go into depth with my mom's story with him but one day I remember my mom coming home from work at 9pm after working from 8am to 8pm on her two feet as she was a cashier at a supermarket. She sat on the ground to eat her food, leaning on a bed which we all were on. They both started arguing and he kicked the plate straight out of her hand kicking her as well. My second brother never forgot this and always speaks about it. He doesn't know what it is he did as he never apologized for all he had done. He never went for help. At least he could have gone to "a meeting". He refused and said nothing was wrong with him. The more challenges were thrown at him, the more my mother got blamed for it and so did I as Was her secret keeper as he once said to me.

There is a lot more but this is just to let you know there is lots of help for many people like this out there. He could have become a better man and changed if he had sought help in counselling or by seeing a therapist. Maybe or maybe not - but one thing I do know: without those seeds that were planted in his head for the man he was, maybe just maybe, he might have been different. This is why you don't make even bad jokes when you are around your friends or a family member when seeing them with an extra beautiful human being (as everyone is beautiful). don't say things like: "he's too handsome. he's not staying with you." or "she is way too beautiful for you. she is definitely cheating on you. No, those jokes sometimes play on those with a weak mind.

It is said when you love something, you cherish it and you treat it well whether it's a human, an animal, a plant or a special flower. Even fish you treat with love.

Life is short. Remember to put yourself in someone else's shoes in all sizes before you cast judgement or even approach them with negativity."

"Spread love and joy and positivity always. Being positive doesn't ever mean you don't have negative thoughts. It really just means you don't let those thoughts control the amazing person you are."

YLEWRAH